THE FOOD OF
INDIA

Authentic Recipes from the Spicy Subcontinent

Recipes by chefs of The Oberoi Group
Photography by Luca Invernizzi Tettoni
Text by Jasjit Purewal, Karen Anand & Jennifer Brennan
Editing by Wendy Hutton
Produced in association with The Oberoi Group

PERIPLUS
EDITIONS

Contents

Part One: Food in India

Three thousand years of tradition and change

India is a vast and ancient land, its recorded history dating back over three thousand years. Yet India today, despite its deeply rooted traditions, is the product of centuries of change, of new ideas, new faiths and new products arriving with traders and invaders, with colonisers and with immigrants fleeing repression elsewhere. The result is a rich tapestry of contradictions and contrasts which never ceases to fascinate.

The astonishing variety of India is reflected in its cuisine, which is regarded by those who have enjoyed genuine Indian food as being among the world's greatest. Like the overall fabric of the land itself, the cuisine of India is the result of countless historical, religious and regional influences.

Stretching from the snowy mountains of Kashmir down to the southern tip of verdant Kerala, from the harsh deserts of Rajasthan in the west across to the remote tribal regions of Assam on the Burmese border, India encompasses an enormous variety of climates which naturally influence the produce available. The Kashmiris, for example, are largely meat eaters since agricultural produce is limited in mountainous regions. In coastal Kerala, where fish abound in the Arabian Sea and "Backwaters" which weave through coconut groves, fish and rich coconut-milk curries predominate.

Religion and caste also play their role in influencing India's cuisines. This is the land which gave rise to two of the world's major religions, Buddhism and Hinduism, and also produced Jainism and Sikhism; faiths from other lands—Islam, Christianity, Zoroastrianism and the Bah'ai faith—have all taken root in the subcontinent. Religious strictures dictate that certain people will not eat beef or pork, or that they are completely vegetarian.

Yet despite the many differences of religion, caste, community and class, there are enough common elements which make it possible to define Indian cuisine. The basis of an Indian meal is a grain, which may be rice, wheat, millet or maize, depending on the region. This is generally eaten with lentils or pulses (*dal*), vegetables and savoury pickles or chutneys. Other dishes of fish, meat or poultry may be added, as well as yogurt. Invariably, the lentils, vegetables and other dishes will be seasoned with spices which not only perform miracles in transforming the taste of the food and sharpening appetites jaded by the heat, but have medicinal values which were recorded in religious texts some three thousand years ago.

Cooking and eating Indian cuisine is thus a discovery of the culture, the richly varied history and the spicy treasures of this fascinating land.

Page 2:
Splendid pageantry and colourful ceremonies are still common throughout India.
Opposite:
The ultimate in Indian dining, an elegantly laid antique table set with thalis of Rajasthani food, while attentive retainers hover nearby.

From the Himalayas to the Tropics

Differing regional tastes in an astonishingly varied subcontinent

India is a land of amazing variety, beginning in the awesome Himalayas in the north and moving on to the great Gangetic plain with its immense and sacred waters, down through the harsh but strangely beautiful deserts of Rajasthan, through plateaux and thick forests, through the Punjab (the "Land of Five Rivers") to the lush green splendour of Kerala—a distance of more than three thousand kilometres.

With its vast land area, India naturally encompasses an enormous variety of climates. As well as its distinct seasonal cycles, India has numerous religions, races and ethnic landscapes which make the subcontinent like a jigsaw of small nations, resulting in a culinary kaleidoscope as colourful as any glass mosaic adorning a Mughal palace.

Generally speaking, rice and wheat are the main staples of the Ayran-influenced north; however, the desert lands of Gujarat and Rajasthan depend far more on millet and maize. In the extreme north lies the fairy-tale land of Kashmir, where racial origins go back to Persia and

A monastery perched on a hillop in the far northern Himalayan district of Ladakh.

Afghanistan. Nestled in the Himalayas, Kashmir, with its almost legendary beauty of crystal clear lakes and snow-clad mountains, depends largely on the valley of Srinagar for agricultural produce. Fruits and nuts are the only real crops of Kashmir, so both Hindus and Muslims depend on diet rich in meat.

Kashmiri food is characterised by its subtle blending of fragrant spices (especially the world's most expensive spice, saffron), by its richness (often the result of ground nuts or poppy seeds) and by the use of asafoetida, a resin which adds a distinctive flavour and is also believed to aid digestion.

Some of the most popular Kashmiri foods include lamb marinated in yogurt; mutton slow-cooked in milk and scented with nutmeg; *Roghan Josh*, a rich meat curry and the famous *Goshtaba* or meat loaf, cooked for many hours to an inimitable silky chewy texture. Kashmiri weddings are incomplete without *Mishani* or the "seven courses of lamb", a paradisal spread for meat eaters. A variety of leavened and unleavened breads are an essential part of any Kashmiri meal.

The Gangetic plain in the middle and eastern part of India is both a rice and wheat-eating belt, although millet and maize are used in some areas by the lower-middle classes. The normal meal in this region consists of plain rice accompanied by vegetables sautéed with spices, *dal,* unleavened bread (either dry-fried on a griddle or deep fried in oil), plain yogurt and a sweet which is normally milk based. Chutney and pickles are common accompaniments, while fruit is enjoyed in season. Meats and fish are consumed mostly by the more affluent middle class and are not a regular part of the diet, except in the east and northeast.

The coastline of Kerala is backed by a network of canals known as the Backwaters, their edges fringed by endless coconut groves.

The east, with its proximity to the Bay of Bengal and its numerous ponds and rivers, is the area where there is the highest fish consumption. This is the only part of India—with the exception of the Kerala coast—where fish is the most popular food. This eastern belt of India, with its large and fertile alluvial lands, is a rice-growing region, so it is not surprising that this is the staple grain.

There are two distinct styles of cooking in Bengal. East Bengal (now Bangladesh) prefers its fish from large rivers, while the west, with Calcutta as its nerve centre, gets its sea food from estuaries and ponds. *Hilsa,* a type of shad which is a member of the herring family, is the most popular fish in the region, despite its numerous small bones. West Bengal is known for its use of poppy seeds and mustard; brownish-black mustard seeds are not only used as a spice but are crushed to make the oil which gives a distinctive flavour to Bengali cooking.

Bengali cuisine is considered elaborate and refined. Bengal is the only place in India where food is served in separate courses, the chronology based on ancient beliefs relating to aiding the digestive process. Bitter leaves and gourd are always served first, followed by rice, *dal,* chutney and the ubiquitous fish. Even the so-called vegetarians of Bengal, who refuse all meat, eat fish and prawns. Some affluent Bengalis also eat meat on occasion. *Mishti Doi* (or sweetened yogurt set in clay pots) is a Bengali delicacy served at the end of the meal, usually with another milk dessert.

The land of South India is essentially composed of solidified iron-rich lava dating back some 50 million years or more. Rice is known to have been grown in this region as far back as 500 B.C., and an efficient irrigation system developed. The Dravidian culture of the south is considerably older than the Aryan culture which influenced the north. Ancient records in Tamil script, which pre-dates even Sanskrit, indicate that this was a highly developed and religious land. Architectural wonders depicting Hindu epics and gods mark the entire land south of the Vindhya mountains, an area where art and music are still preserved and practiced in their traditional forms.

Food, too, retains much of its traditional style in the south and regardless of class, Southern Indians still sit cross-legged on a floor mat to eat from a stainless steel plate (*thali*) or piece of fresh banana leaf.

Rice, the southern staple, is everywhere and appears in many different guises: steamed, puffed, made into paper-thin crepes known as *Dosay* or steamed to form *Idli*. Both *Dosay* and *Idli* are made by soaking rice and *dal* overnight in buttermilk until fermented, then grinding them to make a paste; this is either steamed to make dumplings or *Idli*, or shallow fried to make *Dosay*. These two foods are eaten with different chutneys, vegetables and light *dal* broths known as *Sambar*.

In Karnataka, the central southern state, some wheat variations like *Mandige* exist; this is a delicate dough baked on a heated tile and stuffed with a variety of ingredients including sugar, cardamom powder and shredded coconut. The basic meal consists of vegetables which accompany the universally popular *Dosay*, *Idli* or steamed rice.

Aubergines are a favourite southern vegetable, seasoned with *ghee*, salt, fenugreek and *dal*; roasted in oil; spiced or cooked directly over charcoal. The bitter gourd is another popular vegetable, not always to Western taste; this is salted to remove most of the bitterness, then stuffed with a variety of spices and tied with a string before being fried in oil or cooked with a crude-sugar (*jaggery*) syrup to offset any trace of bitterness.

Relishes abound and are generally pungent. *Balaka* is made of red chillies soaked in salt water, dried and fried in oil to make a crisp and spicy accompaniment. *Papads* or *poppadums*, paper-fine disks of wheat or rice-flour and lentil flour, are crisp fried and eaten together with meals.

Sweets in the south are normally variations of rice. Star of the somewhat limited repertoire of desserts is *Payasam*, consisting of wheat vermicelli, *dal* such as Bengal gram or sometimes sago cooked in sugared milk spiced with cardamom.

Even though largely vegetarian, the south has its hybrid groups like the Kodavas, who cook rice with chunks of meat, serving it with a spicy sesame chutney. Steamed balls of rice constitute *Kadambaputt*, which is eaten with pork cooked with the purplish-black *kokum* fruit, the acidity of which keeps the fat on the meat firm and springy. Popular fish include sardines and a tiny whitebait, crisp fried and eaten whole, bones and all.

The coastal area of Kerala, which has been subjected to foreign influences for thousands of years, is a strong fish and meat-eating region. Jewish settlers came to Kerala as long ago as A.D. 7, bringing with them the notion of slaughtering livestock as humanely as possible so that the meat was acceptable or *kosher* (a concept adopted by Muslims who refer to such food as *halal*).

Syrian Christians escaping persecution at home settled in the southwestern state of Kerala during the 4th century A.D. Not being bound by Hindu prohibitions on beef, Kerala's Christians have developed a number of beef dishes where the meat is tenderised by various means (usually with vinegar or by par-boiling before transforming it into a rich coconut-milk curry). They are also renowned for their wild duck dishes, where the duck is either cooked to make a curry or stuffed and roasted, the latter being a traditional Christmas dish. Wild boar, cooked with a tangy *masala* or pickled with oil, is another famous Syrian Christian dish.

The Muslims of Kerala love their soups of rice and wheat laced with spices and coconut milk. *Kiskiya*, a whole wheat porridge cooked with minced meat, is an all time favourite.

Apart from the British, other foreigners who established themselves in India were the Portuguese, who remained in their colony of Goa, north of Kerala, from the 16th century until after Indian independence from the British, finally quitting in 1961. Goans are known for their use of vinegar and *kokum* fruit (other Indians add sourness with tamarind, lime juice, dried mango powder or, in some areas, *kokum*) as well as for their love of fiery chillies. Classic examples of Goan cuisine are the pork curry, *Vindaloo*, which gets its name from the Portuguese words for vinegar and garlic, and Sorpotel, a sour hot curry of pork, liver and pig's blood. Portuguese priests are thought to have introduced

Opposite:
A southern Indian vegetarian thali with a range of spiced vegetables, soup, pickle, rice, breads, banana and dessert

Left:
Offerings of coconut, bananas, flowers and incense on display at a market stall in a typical southern Indian village.

The huge airy room just off a kitchen in this Portuguese-style Goan home is reminiscent of a leisurely past.

Zoroastrians came in large numbers to settle in India when they were hounded out of Persia as far back as A.D. 850. Parsis, as they are now known, settled largely in Gujarat. They brought with them a strong meat-eating tradition and a love of egg dishes, raisins, nuts, butter and cream. They inevitably absorbed Gujarati influences and a hybrid cuisine developed. One of the most famous of these dishes is the Parsi fish steamed in banana-leaf packets. Another widely known Parsi dish is *Dhansak*, a one-pot meal combining several types of *dal* with spices, meat and vegetables.

Islam swept into India as long ago as the 8th century, but it was not until the 16th century that the Muslims gained control over large parts of northern India, converting millions of

the art of distillation, thus giving birth to the famous Goan *feni*, which is distilled from the fermented sap of the cashew nut and the coconut palm.

Gujarat is the haven of vegetarians. Millet, barley and wheat are equally loved, and snacks are the Gujarati art-form. *Nasto* is made from Bengal-gram flour (*besan*) mixed with an assortment of spices and fried. *Chevda* or beaten rice is fried and mixed with salt, spices, almonds, raisins and peanuts.

people to their faith. The Mughul dynasties, which ruled various independent states of pre-Independence India, upstaged the mainstream Hindu culture and cuisine significantly. New flavours, rich relishes, meats with cream and butter sauces, dates, nuts and delectable sweets were the hallmarks of a cuisine which is now widely known and famed for its exotic, non-vegetarian food, rich and aromatic with the memories and music of a far-distant land.

The Indian Food Ethos

In India, philosophy and food are inseparable

Sita, the wife of the Hindu god, Rama, and a legendary symbol of purity, apparently loved her venison and rice, washing it down frequently with *maireya,* a special wine. So what was the good and chaste deity of the Brahmins doing with these now forbidden foods? Yet another Indian epic tells us of how the Brahmins were honoured by kings in great feasts where they were fed pork and venison. The great Indian epics, the Ramayana and the Mahabharata, go back millennia. Obviously, eating traditions underwent a sharp change at some time in history so that today, many of the followers of those very gods are now staunch vegetarians and teetotallers, making India the largest country of vegetarians in the world.

The Vedas, ancient historical and religious texts dating from from 1700–1500 B.C., set the framework for what is broadly known as Hindu culture. They record the civilisation of the Aryans or nomadic tribes from the upper Urals, who travelled as far east as India on one side and as far west as Ireland on the other. Most Hindu food practices were influenced by the Aryans, beginning in the north and the northwest of India and gradually spreading all over the country.

The Aryans did not treat food simply as a means to physical sustenance but saw it as part of a cosmic circle, their dictum being "the food that man eats and his universe must be in harmony." Food, they believed, gave rise to three products: those which needed expulsion, those which were absorbed into the flesh and those which were transformed into thought or mind. The last were the finest and rarest of foods and referred to as *manas.* The term *prasad* was used for food left over from offerings to the gods, food which was considered pure nectar, which left no trace and which maintained man's spirituality.

Food was classified into different categories: cereals, pulses, vegetables, fruit, spices, milk products, animal meats and alcoholic beverages. Guidelines for consumption of these foods were drawn up, including which foods were holy or unholy, which foods were required for a particular religious practice or season and the order in which various foods should be consumed.

This was the time when *ghee* or clarified butter emerged as a popular cooking medium because of its associations with purity, as it was used in religious sacrifices and offerings. Most traditional Indian cooking in the north still uses cholesterol-high *ghee,* although modern Indians have switched to cooking oil. In the past, cooking oils were generally looked down upon as an inferior cooking medium.

Even Indian gods are believed to be tempted by earthly food.

leaf as a ritual act of purification before eating.

According to Hindu tradition, food was systematically arranged on the banana leaf. Even though archaeology confirms the existence of sophisticated cooking and eating dishes, eating from banana leaves was encouraged to prevent cross pollution. It is believed that food should never be eaten standing up, lying down or eaten off the lap. Sitting on the ground, facing east or north and eating in total silence were all encouraged.

Portions of food were saved for Brahmins, dogs and serpents, and laid outside for crows who were seen as messengers to the world of spirits. The householder was expected to first feed any guests, pregnant women, infants, the aged and the sick before he sat down to eat.

Eating with the fingers is the norm, the use of cutlery being a very recent and western influence. Only the right hand should be used while eating because the left hand was reserved for certain bodily functions. Washing hands when entering a home and especially before eating is uniformly practiced.

In the south, the Dravidians pre-date the Aryans and are therefore seen as being culturally more "pure" than people from the north. The pre-Aryan southerners did not mind eating meat and their high priests also consumed meat and alcohol. At this time, black pepper was used by the Dravidians to make a tangy sauce eaten with meat, known as *kari*: The word was later anglicised to "curry", eventually coming to mean any dish with a spicy sauce.

Marriage, pregnancy, death and birth are all associated with certain foods. Special foods, like rice

The Aryans introduced many practices which made food both a physical and spiritual activity in human lives. Pollution is an important concept, and it would be unthinkable for a cook or a housewife to taste any dish during preparation. Water must never be sipped from a glass but poured into one's mouth, since saliva can be polluting. Water used for rinsing the mouth should not be swallowed. Many people sprinkle water around their *thali* or banana stained with turmeric, grains of barley, parched grains and *ghee* are a must for ceremonial events like weddings. Pregnancies are subject to do's and don'ts and even after the birth, special rich foods and herbal cooking is emphasised for the lactating mother. A child's first tasting of food, called *annaprasan* (literally "tasting grain"), is an event for celebration when a concoction of boiled rice, milk, sugar and honey is introduced as the first solid food. Milk products, certain *dal*, Bengal gram powder and turmeric are not used during death and mourning because they are all considered auspicious foods.

Free communal meals are served to literally thousands of guests at religious festivals.

Even abstinence from food or fasting is a critical Hindu ritual. Partial fasts carried out for purification demand that certain foods be avoided, but total abstinence is rare. Serving *langar* or free food to thousands of people in temples or at religious festivals, where sharing and eating together occurs on an almost unimaginable scale, is a widespread and uniquely Indian eating practice where the disposable banana leaf plate is essential.

Ancient food habits were altered by religion and trade, through occupation and invasion, with Indian cuisines becoming more varied and vibrant. Religion was a major influence in changing food habits, with Buddhism and Jainism starting the first indigenous movements which challenged Hindu practices.

Abstinence, austerity and simplicity were the tenets of changes which questioned, amongst other things, the eating of meat. Jainism underlined the importance of "innocent" foods and vegetarianism was born. Sikhism followed to reaffirm simplicity, with tobacco and alcohol becoming inscribed targets.

Finally, colonial India left its marks on both the food and eating practices. In middle-class homes, the dining table replaced the kitchen floor and porcelain, the banana leaf. Fingers gave way to knives, forks and other Western niceties. Lovers of Indian food point out that it cannot be eaten easily with cutlery, since the unleavened bread needs to be broken by hand and vegetables and *dal* should be kneaded into the rice. Others with a more poetic turn of phrase claim that eating Indian food with cutlery is like making love through an interpreter.

The Great Spice Bazaar

Masalas and medicines: India's amazingly versatile spices

Walk into an Indian home at meal time, or into a good Indian restaurant, and you will be engulfed by a wave of heavenly aromas. Without doubt, the most distinctive feature of Indian food is its creative combination of spices which give an inimitable flavour and aroma. The use of spices in India was recorded in Sanskrit texts 3,000 years ago. The Ayurveda, an ancient treatise on health which covers aspects of both mental and physical health, sets out principles for healthy living; included are lists of various spices, their medicinal properties detailed.

Spices have been used for their medicinal properties as well as for flavouring and preservation since time immemorial.

So great was the importance of spices for seasoning, as preservatives and as medicine—not just in India but throughout the world—that the search for their source pushed the Europeans into the Age of Exploration in the 15th century.

Given their long familiarity with spices, it is not surprising that Indian cooks use them as skillfully as an artist the colours of his palette. "Spices", in a culinary sense, embraces dried seeds, berries, bark, rhizomes, flowers, leaves and chillies. Each spice has its own culinary and medicinal properties; some are used primarily for their flavour, others for the exquisite aroma they add. Certain spices are used whole, others always ground into powder; some go superbly with meat but would overpower more delicate fish and vegetable dishes. Only a few spices (cardamom, saffron and cinnamon) are used for desserts, yet these same spices also appear in meat dishes. It seems little short of miraculous that the Indian cook remembers (for recipes are almost never written down) which spices to use and in what combination.

Any combination of spices is referred to as a *masala*. The most widely used—a fragrant combination of dark, pungent spices including cinnamon, cloves, black pepper and cardamom, with the optional addition of nutmeg, mace and saffron in northern regions—is known as *garam masala*.

With such tremendous climatic variations in India, certain spices grow only in particular regions. While cardamoms, cloves and peppers are harvested mainly in the south, Rajasthan, Kashmir and Gujarat also grow many spices, with regional market places piling up freshly ground red chilli powder alongside vivid yellow turmeric, which is flanked by mounds of cardamoms and black peppers.

The most colourful stall in the market, the spice merchant, is but a poor second to the fields where turmeric and red chillies are harvested and dried. In the stark yellow deserts of Rajasthan, the spice fields have a colourful splendour quite their own. One of the glorious sights of Kashmir is fields of purplish-blue crocuses, whose fine thread-like orange stigmas are harvested in October and November.

Although India is modernising and neat plastic packets of spices can be bought all over the country, many housewives still prefer to buy loose spices from the huge piles offered by the spice merchant and grind their spices just before cooking.

But what of "curry powder", that ingredient which some Western cooks consider the basis of all Indian curries? No Indian cook would dream of using the same combination of spices for all types of food. There are specific combinations of whole or ground spices (*masala*) for certain dishes, but these are never used alone. Curry powder as sold outside India was initially developed in Madras for nostalgic British trying to re-capture the flavours of India after they returned home.

The medicinal properties of spices are always taken into account when food is prepared, as well as the interaction of each spice with the natural properties of a particular vegetable or *dal*. Some vegetables and *dals* are supposed to create gas in the body, so asafoetida, cinnamon and cumin are used to balance this. Turmeric is an antiseptic and drunk mixed with hot milk to check internal haemorrhages. Its regular use in everyday foods helps prevent internal wounds and infections.

Clove, fennel and cardamom tea has many benefits, especially for the common cold, upset stomach and chill. Cloves are used for gum and teeth infections and inflammations. Saffron boiled in milk is supposed to check anaemia and help restore strength. Ginger crushed with honey is sure to cure the worst cough and garlic will not only keep cholesterol levels down but reduce the ill effects of toxins in the body. Fenugreek seeds roasted in oil help arthritic pains, asafoetida roasted on an iron griddle and mixed with salt helps clear gastric disorders. Every Indian home uses spices for natural cures, the recipes being uniform and passed down for countless generations from the ancient religious texts.

Nutmegs being weighed in the wholesale spice maket of Cochin.

The Honoured Guest

Indian hospitality is justifiably legendary

The hospitality of Indians, no matter how humble or how lavish their homes, is little short of overwhelming. Part of the explanation for this is that the guest is still seen as an evocation of God and his arrival considered an auspicious event. *Athithya*, a sacred word which means serving a guest, is an important part of a man's social duties and from the Vedic times, guests were ceremoniously received with the traditional yogurt, milk, honey and sugar.

In a land of many poor households, this attitude is still strong, especially in the countryside. Guest is a generic term for anyone who visits and total strangers coming into a village or family are treated with respect; any visitor, even to a poor village, is served water and something sweet. During a festival in some villages in the Punjab, doors are left open to any guest who enters, and they are fed, regardless of class or cast.

Three distinct meal times mark eating patterns everywhere. Breakfast, lunch (which is a far more elaborate meal than Western sandwich lunches) and dinner are uniform. Traditionally, guests would visit only on special occasions and festivals, but in modern India and especially among the middle and upper classes, inviting friends for a meal is now a common social practice.

Food is generally served on a banana leaf or a stainless steel *thali*. Washing the hands before meals is an important ritual, since Indians generally use their fingers to eat and the meal is eaten squatting down, usually on the kitchen floor. A small straw mat is placed for sitting and the *thali* or banana leaf is laid in front of the mat, either on the floor or on a low stool.

Families eat together, except for the mother or wife who serves the meal. In middle-class homes, however, this role is taken over by the household help. The family normally sits in a straight line and the women of the household serve and refill the *thali* repeatedly. As it is considered discourteous and unclean to serve while eating, the mother or wife serving in a traditional household will not eat until the men have finished. Female guests can either be served with the men or eat with the women later.

Water is sprinkled around the banana leaf or *thali* to purify it before beginning a meal. The *thali* contains all the courses of the meal, but there is usually an order in which the food is eaten. The first mouthfuls of rice are eaten with *ghee* or chutney and spicy additives. *Dal* is served along with a variety of dry-cooked vegetables seasoned with different spices and garnishes. *Papads* and relishes are replenished, as are the *dal* and rice. The best portions of fish and meat are always offered to the

PART ONE: FOOD IN INDIA

A selection of fragrant nibbles constituting supari, *served in a quaint antique brass box.*

southern practice, *paan* is now eaten at all times of the day all the way up to the northeast. Artistically crafted *paan* containers or *pandaan* in copper, brass and silver hold the different ingredients. *Paan* concoctions have grown elaborate and up to 15 condiments can be added, including the infamous but popular *zarda,* or chewing tobacco. The *pandaans* are carefully perforated to allow circulation and come together with a tool designed for slicing the areca nut; these are often exquisitely designed in the shape of celestial figures or adorned with amorous carvings. Spittoons to carry the residue of the saliva

guest; in Bengal, this would be the head of the fish, regarded as the choicest portion. *Roti* or unleavened bread, *puri* (fried puffed wheat bread) and *paratha* (shallow-fried wheat bread) are common in the north and are eaten with *dal* and vegetables. The sweet, which is milk based, completes the meal, although in the south it is followed by rice with curds or buttermilk which are believed to soothe the stomach after a spicy meal.

Finally, *paan* or the betel leaf and its seasonings adds that very Indian touch to *athithiya*, apart from acting as a digestive. This leaf is chewed along with a slice of areca nut, a dab of slaked lime and a smear of *katha* paste (another wood extract). Primarily a

and chewed leaf are elaborate vessels of metal. The betel quid can mean many things: hospitality; moral and legal commitment; a digestive and a fitting end to the remarkable hospitality displayed during a meal.

An alternative digestive to *paan* is the delightful mixtures of spices (especially aniseed-flavoured fennel), dried fruits (sometimes coated with silver leaf), tiny sugar-coated balls, sugar crystals drenched with rose essence and other tangy combinations known collectively as *supari*. So popular is this that airlines within India offer passengers the choice of boiled sweets or tiny packets of *supari*, continuing the tradition of honouring a guest.

The Raj Revisited

Curry tiffins and afternoon tea: culinary remnants of the colonial era

The Indian army officer strides into the Officer's Club. It is still exactly the same as it was during the colonial era: dusty trophies, stuffed animal heads mounted on the walls, tattered flags stirring softly in the breeze from the *punkahs* (fans). He reads the newspapers (in English, of course) and then lunches on roast lamb or chicken rissoles, gravy, peas and potatoes.

The period of colonial rule has left an indelible impact on both India and Britain. After the initial clashes between the British and the peoples of the Indian subcontinent, the Raj sought first to exploit, then to rule and finally, to administer. At that stage, both parties perceived their relationship as "something to be put up with, to be endured". What astounded both the British and the Indians was that after their long and sometimes acrimonious relationship, neither realised that its subsequent shattering would inflict upon both parties a mutual sense of loss. As the wounds healed, this sentiment resolved into a lasting affection, loyalty and the incorporation of romantic and fanciful selections of each others' language and customs. This is particularly so in relation to the preparation and consumption of food and its attendant rituals.

The entire historical episode was, in fact, gastronomically inspired. For the English, it all began with their attempts to corner the spice trade. Although they were originally focussed on the fabled "East Indies", they found the Indian subcontinent a more bountiful source of valuable spices and foodstuffs. By the 16th century, the English already employed many of these exotic adjuncts to food and medicine at home, regarding them as indispensable.

The irony was that by the 19th century, when wives and families joined their menfolk in India, British food had reverted to plain and pedestrian, although lavish in quantity and display. It was now the turn of the Indians to enliven and "spice" it again. This devolved, most naturally, though the colonialists' own kitchens.

The Indian cooks prepared, to the best of their abilities, the alien food that the foreign *memsahibs*

The British colonials were joined by their wives in India only during the 19th century.

ordered them to produce. Often these dishes were a dismal failure, to the chagrin of the diners and the exasperation of the cook or *khansamer*; other times it was transmogrified into strange preparations neither English nor Indian, but with a nod to both. Sometimes, however, the dishes transcended their disparate roots and became the forerunners of a remarkably successfuly culinary fusion.

Indian spices were frequently used by cooks to preserve leftover meats. These were subsequently presented as entrees with the satanic adjective "devilled", that is to say, spiced with chillies, mustard seeds, vinegar and other natural preservatives. The results were hot, tangy and piquant dishes which inspired and titillated palates enervated by the monotony of colonial life and tropical weather.

In the manner of tourists today, the homebound British sought to take with them items to remind them of "the Jewel in the Crown". As their palates had gradually become accustomed to the impact of spiced and pungent foods, such as Indian *chatnis*—condiments of herbs, spices, vegetables and chillies—they requested that these preparations be cooked to preserve them in the manner of Indian pickles, albeit with the more palate-pleasing addition of sugar. The *sahibs* and *memsahibs* hoped that these concoctions would survive the voyage home and be useful in leavening the stodginess of "home food", evoking echoes of the exotic dishes of which they had become enamored. So, in the English tradition of "putting up" or "bottling", these *chatnis* turned into relishes and sauces with the flavour of the tropics and the instant memory of India within their glass containers. Eventually, there ensued a panoply of bottled chutneys which graced the shelves of every major British grocer.

The most remarkable Anglicisation of local food was the result of British inattentiveness to the finer details of Indian cooking; most *memsahibs* spent no time in their kitchens in any case. They used the word "curry" as a generic term for any sauced dish of hot, spiced meats, fish and/or vegetables. (The name curry is generally agreed to be a corruption of the Tamil word for sauce, *kari*.) Misunderstanding the purpose of the almost limitless combinations of spices in the *masalas* individually blended to enhance the main ingredients of each preparation, the British came up with curry powder—a one-chord reproduction of Indian spicing—which guaranteed that any dish would taste like the other. And as the "old *kohais*" or India hands decreed "the hottah the bettah!", curry powder became the principal Anglo-Indian contribution to culinary lore and bedevilled Indian cuisine in the eyes of much of the world for years to come.

Countless British children—myself included—were brought up in India on a regime of such comforting nursery dishes as kedgeree, Anglicised from its original rice and lentil mixture (*kichidee*) with the delicious additions of smoked fish, onions and hard-boiled eggs. Mulligatawny soup was another delight, translated from the traditional rather watery version of "pepper water" (*mooloogoo thani*) to a thick, spiced soup of lentils and vegetables, often based on chicken stock.

The Indian custom of a light snack or repast, called *tiffin*, eventually came to mean lunch in the middle of the day for the British. While the tea bush was growing wild in Assam around 1820, in 1841 tea plants from China were transplanted by the Raj to nearby Darjeeling and, by 1866, there were some 10,000 acres of plants. Eventually, tea became the national Indian beverage with *char wallahs* selling it, freshly brewed, in the streets and on railway station platforms. Upper-class Indians embraced the English customs of afternoon teas, complete with sandwiches and cakes, usually accompanied by Indian snacks as well.

By the time the Raj left India, generations of Indian cooks knew how to prepare cutlets, croquettes, sausages, cakes, puddings, jams and biscuits. They were hired by clubs, hotels and upper-income families and continued cooking these dishes.

In India today, in upper-class homes, in private clubs and military clubs, Anglo-Indian food is as deeply entrenched as ever. And the departed Raj?

Anglicised Indian food was standard fare in the dak *bungalows where travelling colonials were obliged to stay.*

We invite each other to Sunday curry *tiffins* or duck into Indian restaurants and sigh with sentimentality as we pile our plates high with mutton *saag, mutter pilau* and *tandoori* chicken with stacks of *chapatis*, towers of *papads* (*poppadums*), fresh mint and bottled mango chutneys washed down with pints of Taj beer. And with the perversity of human nature, both the Indians and the British look back fondly to "The Good Old Days".—*Jennifer Brennan*

At Home and Abroad

The search for authentic regional cuisines
is not always easy

It is undisputed among gourmets that Indian food ranks as one of the world's greatest cuisines. However, like many other fine cuisines, it does not always travel well, neither abroad nor within its vast homeland. Visitors to India, who normally eat in their hotels—unless they are fortunate enough to have Indian friends invite them into their homes or into some of the interesting regional restaurants—are likely to come away from the country without any idea of the astonishing regional variety of food and of the excellence of home-style cooking.

Ironically, it is usually easier to find regional Indian food in restaurants abroad than in restaurants in India.

They will probably also leave convinced that *tandoori* food is India's most popular, despite the fact that it's virtually impossible to find a clay *tandoor* oven in an Indian home and that this style of cooking originates in just one region of India, the northwest or Punjab. The current wide-spread popularity of *tandoori* foods in restaurants is a relatively recent phenomenon and largely attributable to the fact the the Punjabis are among the most mobile of India's ethnic groups and enjoy eating their own food when they go out. Other affluent Indians, who eat their own style of cuisine regularly at home, like to try something different when they dine out and find that the *tandoori* food of the Punjabis is very much to their taste

Home food is influenced by such factors as climate, nutritional balance and religion. "Home food" throughout the country is usually simple fare where rice, bread such as *chapati* and *dal* constitute the core of the meal. Each region and each household then adds its distinctive touch with the vegetables, the meat and fish and the "ticklers" (pickles, crunchy *papads* and yogurt-based salads, or *raita)*.

Although there are thousands of wonderful Indian recipes, most are oral, handed down from mother to daughter. Wealthy families and the Maharajas patronised a certain style of cuisine which was unique and where cooks were employed often to create and cook just a single dish in their lifetime. In Lucknow, a *nawab* discovered the technique of slow cooking with steam inside the pot (*dum*), with the lid sealed with dough and hot coals place on top. A chain of hotels introduced this type of cuisine to a broader market within India, after much research in tracking down the often illiterate old cooks. Similarly, much work was done to find and standardise the variety of dishes which come from the Malabar Coast of Southwest India.

There is a slow but growing emergence of small chef-proprietor restaurants throughout India today. The major constraint here is financial, as real estate in major Indian cities like Bombay and Delhi is prohibitive. What draws people from all backgrounds to these eateries is the freshness and consistency of the food. Unfortunately, these places—such as the seafood restaurants and Gujarati *thali* houses in Bombay and the South Indian fast food outlets or *darshinis* in Bangalore—remain largely inaccessible to the foreign traveller. Some top Indian hotels, however, aware of criticism of the domination of Punjabi-style cuisine, are now starting to offer menus that reflect the enormous variety of India's culinary heritage on their menus.

Indian food abroad is a different matter. Although "curry" has been around in Britian since the days of the Raj, it was, for many years, just a spicy alternative to bland British fare and bore little resemblance to anything produced in Indian homes. During the 1970s, however, a genuine interest and awareness of food developed and Indian restaurants started becoming aware of the new up-market demands for authenticity, freshness and attractive decor. There were Indian cookery programmes on television; ingredients like Basmati rice, whole spices, fresh ginger, coriander leaves and curry pastes began to appear on supermarket shelves and eating authentic Indian food became trendy.

This story has been repeated in places as far flung as Hong Kong, Sydney and San Francisco. Indian restaurants in these cities initially catered only to Indians, but as general food awareness increased, so did the number of restaurants where sensitivity in terms of both the food and the decor play an essential role. And with the world-wide trend of "fusion cuisine", where elements of one culinary style are blended with another, one can expect the use of Indian spice blends or *masalas* and Indian vegetables to creep in everywhere. Indian cuisine, despite its ancient traditions, is still evolving and creating new dishes. Travellers look forward to the day when the best of India's regional cuisines will be easily avai-lable in the country's better restaurants and hotels.—*Karen Anand*

Northern Indan food is found in almost all elegant restaurants in India.

Part Two: The Indian Kitchen

A place of sanctity and
surprising simplicity

The traditional Indian kitchen was an area of sanctity with many taboos on who could enter, how they should be dressed and how pollution must be avoided. Most of this has changed today, although the importance of the Indian hearth within the home is still paramount.

Millions of Indian kitchens are essentially very simple, with the stove set in the centre. Although this stove, or *chula,* is often heated by charcoal, in the countryside, dried cow-dung cakes and wood shavings are still widely used. Dried dung is actually considered more "pure" than any other type of fuel and provides a gentle heat ideal for slow cooking. Modern gas stoves have replaced the *chula* in many middle-class urban homes.

Cooking ranges and electric gadgets, such as rice cookers and blenders, are slowly appearing in urban Indian homes, but since many of these households can afford kitchen help, traditional methods are preserved for taste and authenticity.

Since the *chula* is normally placed on the floor, most women cook sitting down on a small wooden stool. For this reason, shoes—which might bring in dirt from the outside—are rarely allowed into a tra-

ditional Indian kitchen.

A large wok-like utensil, the *kadai,* is used for frying and sautéing. The *kadai,* which is made of iron, brass or aluminium, is slightly deeper than a wok, but the latter makes an excellent substitute.

For cooking rice and curries, a flat-lidded, straight-sided pan known as a *degchi* is used. These were traditionally made of lined brass, but are now generally made of aluminium and very inexpensive, even if less attractive.

Almost any saucepan can be used for cooking Indian dishes, but take care to choose one that has a non-reactive lining, since many dishes contain acid. Nonstick saucepans are ideal for Indian food as they avoid the problem of spices sticking on the bottom and allow you to use less oil when frying.

Indian breads are rolled out with a wooden rolling pin on a flat circular stone slab or wooden board and cooked on a heavy iron griddle, or *tawa.* A heavy cast-iron frying pan or griddle makes a good substitute.

Spices, various seasonings such as ginger, garlic and onions, as well as grains such as rice and lentils are ground at home. The grinding stone is such an important symbol of the hearth and home that in

Opposite:
Most spices are bought whole and freshly ground at home, using a granite slab or mortar and pestle.
Left:
A lined copper kadai *for frying and sautéing.*

some areas of the country, the bride stands on a grinding stone during part of the wedding ceremony, symbolising that she is now mistress of her own household.

Small amounts of spices are crushed just before cooking, either on a flat granite slab or, in the south, in a black stone concave bowl. Modern cooks will find a small coffee grinder kept specially for the task of grinding spices does the job far more quickly and effortlessly. Large slabs of granite with a granite rolling pin are used for grinding large amounts of seasonings or grain. The electric food processor is a welcome substitute for the grinding stone and is ideal for large amounts of ingredients.

Above:
Traditional granite grinding slab.
Bottom right:
An old fuel stove with a griddle or tawa *for cooking* chapati.

Steaming utensils for making *Idli* in the south and *Farsan* in Gujarat are common, some of them now made to fit into pressure cookers. Other regional cuisines demand special utensils, such as the cylindrical clay ovens, or *tandoor,* used to bake Mughul-style breads and meats in the north. In Kashmir, samovars bubble all day long, brewing the favourite aromatic green tea, *kahwah*, together with green cardamoms and almonds.

Coconut graters are essential items in Bengali and southern Indian kitchens. A serrated iron disc mounted on wood, and often hand-cranked, is used for removing the fibres from the coconut as well as for shredding and grating the flesh. Split bamboo baskets are used for straining the coconut milk and also serve as multi-purpose sieves. They are particularly attractive in the northeast, where they are intricately woven and come in all sizes.

In meat-eating homes of the north and south, solid wooden chopping blocks and cleavers are used. An all-purpose Chinese cleaver and thick wooden board are useful additions to any kitchen where Indian food is to be prepared. Cooking ladles, generally of steel or aluminium with rounded ends, are used for stirring *dal* and curries, while small wire mesh baskets with long wooden handles are used to retrieve items after deep frying. Simple but attractive unglazed eathernware bowls are used for setting yogurt; any glass or ceramic bowl or jar can be used instead.

Eating utensils are uniform across India, with the stainless steel *thali* or tray set with a variety of small bowls for curries, *dal* and yogurt. The old *thali* were made of brass, bell metal or silver, but stainless steel is preferred today because it is cheap and easy to clean. Porcelain and melamine tableware have invaded middle-class homes everywhere, yet the stainless steel *thali* is still the most common eating plate. Many Indians prefer to eat with their right hand, believing that the food actually tastes better or that cutlery is unhygenic. Despite this, many middle-class families use a spoon and fork at mealtimes.

In the southern and eastern areas of India, one versatile utensil is invariably found during festivals and weddings: a square of freshly picked banana leaf, which makes the perfect, biodegradable disposable plate.

Cooking Methods

*Indian cuisine is actually easier
to prepare than it sounds*

Although Indian cuisine involves using an often-complex blending of spices and sometimes two or three different cooking methods during the preparation of a single dish, it is very much easier than it sounds.

Most Indian dishes involve the use of **spices**, and as each spice takes a different amount of time to release its flavour and aroma, it is important to follow the correct order given when adding spices to the cooking pan. To be sure of maximum flavour and aroma, always buy whole spices and grind them just before cooking. First heat the spices gently in a dry pan, shaking frequently, until they start to smell fragrant, taking care they do not burn. Cool slightly, then grind in a small electric grinder.

Spices are then usually gently sautéed in oil or *ghee*, either alone or together with meat or vegetables. Be sure to keep the temperature low and to keep stirring the spices so they do not stick to the bottom of the pan. Using plenty of oil or *ghee* helps ensure the spices do not stick; if you're health conscious, you might like to pour off any excess oil once the spices are cooked, or use a non-stick pan.

Many vegetable dishes and curries are, after the initial *bhuna* or sautéing stage, simmered over very low heat on the top of the stove. The pan is often kept covered to ensure that the aromas do not escape. An exception to this is when **coconut** milk is used, as it is in a number of southern Indian dishes. As coconut milk tends to curdle or break apart easily, it should always be brought to the boil slowly, stirring frequently and lifting up the milk with a large ladle, pouring it back down into the pan. Once it has come to the boil, it should always be simmered uncovered.

Additional seasoning is often added just before the food is served. This may be as simple as a sprinkle of aromatic sweet *garam masala*, or, especially in southern India, the addition of some fried brown mustard seeds, dried chillies and curry leaves. Interestingly, this stage is known as "tempering", after the Portuguese *temperado*, meaning "to season".

Before it is used in Indian dishes, yogurt is often vigorously stirred to ensure that the whey is properly incorporated with the curds; this is referred to as **whipped yogurt**. Yogurt is also frequently hung to drain off some of the whey and obtain thicker curds. Although this is done using cheesecloth or muslin fabric in India, cooks elsewhere may find an easier method is to put the yogurt in a paper-lined coffee filter and set the cone-shaped device over a jar. The whey will drip through, leaving the curds in the filter. This is **hung yogurt**, which is preferred for cooking, as it does not change its texture.

Indian Ingredients

A treasure trove of exotic spices and seasonings

Asafoetida

Carom

Black Cardamom

ASAFOETIDA: This strong-smelling gum derived from a Persian plant is believed to aid digestion. Known in India as *hing*, it is used in very small amounts—either a pea-sized chunk of resin or, more commonly, a pinch of powdered asafoetida—and gives a unique flavour to certain dishes.

CAROM: The botanical name for this spice, which comes from the same family as cummin and parsley, is *Carum ajowan*. Known as carom or bishop's weed in the West, it is called *ajwain* in India. The flavour is similar to caraway with overtones of thyme; it is worth trying to locate this spice as its use makes a subtle difference to the final flavour.

BESAN: Flour made from Bengal gram or *channa dal*, sometimes referred to as gram flour. *Besan* is used to make batter for vegetables or fish, or to thicken and add flavour to other dishes.

CARDAMOM: Two types of cardamom are used in India. The more common are small, greenish or straw-coloured pods containing a dozen or so tiny, intensely aromatic black seeds. Large black cardamom pods, which are at least six times the size of the green cardamoms, are used in some northern Indian dishes. Do not buy ground cardamom as it is virtually flavourless compared with the heavenly fragrance of the freshly crushed whole spice.

CHILLI: Many different varieties of chillies are used in India, although paradoxically, they are used fresh only in their unripe green state. The majority of ripe red chillies—literally tonnes of them—are dried and a large percentage ground to make chilli powder. Dried chillies should be cut or broken into pieces and soaked in hot water for about 10 minutes to soften them before grinding or blending; in the case of Goan recipes, the chillies should be soaked in vinegar rather than water. If you want to reduce the heat without loosing the flavour, discard some or all of the seeds.

CHIRONJI NUTS: Small brownish nuts which look a little like large sunflower seeds, these are sometimes ground together with other nuts, such as cashews or almonds, or with white poppy seeds to enrich some dishes. The flavour is similar to that of hazelnuts, although they are perhaps best substituted with a mixture of both hazelnuts and almonds.

CINNAMON: True cinnamon comes from the fragrant bark of a tree native to Sri Lanka, and is lighter in colour, thinner and more expensive than cassia bark, which is often sold as cinnamon. The latter has a slightly sweeter flavour than cinnamon, but makes an acceptable substitute. Do not use powdered cinnamon as a substitute where cinnamon sticks are called for. **Cinnamon leaf** or *tej patta*, which comes from a tree related to the cinnamon and cassia, is used in some dishes. Bay leaves make an acceptable substitute.

CLOVES: Although native to the Moluccan islands of Indonesia, cloves have been grown in India for centuries. Use the whole, dark brown nail-shaped spice rather than powdered cloves.

CORIANDER: The small round beige **seeds** of the coriander plant are perhaps the most widely used spice in India and are always ground before use. Fresh **coriander leaves** are used as a herb and are increasingly available in the West, especially in Chinese or Southeast Asian shops. Fresh coriander is often known abroad as *cilantro* or "Chinese parsley".

CUMIN: Used either whole or ground to make a powder, cumin seed (*jeera*) is believed to aid digestion and is one of the most frequently used spices. Less common is the so-called **black cumin** (*kala jeera*), which is not related to cumin at all.

CURRY LEAF: An important herb in southern Indian cooking, this small, dark green leaf has a distinctive flavour which is sadly missing from the dried herb. When a sprig of curry leaves is specified in a recipe, this means about 8–12 individual leaves.

DAL: Often referred to as "dhal" in English, this term covers a variety of lentils. The major ones are: *channa dal* or **Bengal gram**, which resembles a small yellow pea and is often sold split and used as a seasoning; *moong dal*, the small green pea which is sprouted to make Oriental beansprouts; *urad dal* or **blackgram dal**, which is sold either with its black skin still on or husked, when it is creamy white in colour; *masoor dal*, salmon-pink lentils; *toor*, *tuvar* or *arhar dal*, a pale yellow lentil which is smaller than the Bengal gram and *kabuli channa* or **chickpeas**, known by their Spanish name, *garbanzos*, in some Western countries.

FENNEL: Similar in appearance to cumin although slightly fatter, fennel has a sweet fragrance similar to aniseed. Some Indian cooks wrongly translate *saunf*, the word for fennel, as aniseed, but that spice is not found in India.

FENUGREEK: The almost square, hard yellowish-brown seeds of the fenugreek plant are strongly flavoured. They are generally used whole in southern Indian dishes and are also frequently used in pickles. **Fenugreek leaves**

Green Cardamom

Chillies

Cinnamon

Cumin & Black Cumin

Curry Leaf

Mace

Mustard Oil

Mustard Seeds

are used as a vegetable and because of their rather bitter taste, are usually combined with other greens or with potatoes. Substitute with spinach if fenugreek leaves are not available. Dried fenugreek leaves (*methi*) are sometimes used as a seasoning; one particular variety, *kassori methi*, is popular in Northwest Frontier food. Try to locate dried *methi* in Indian shops for the distinctive difference it makes to the final flavour.

GARAM MASALA: A blend of several strongly aromatic spices designed to add flavour and fragrance to meat dishes. Powdered *garam masala* can be bought from any store specialising in spices. You can make your own by grinding whole spices (page 39); store it in a covered jar in the deep-freeze for maximum flavour after grinding.

GARLIC: Garlic is widely used both as a flavouring and for its medicinal qualites. It is often pounded or puréed before use in curries. Many middle-class Indian cooks now buy packets or jars of crushed garlic or garlic-ginger paste; these are often available in the West and should be refrigerated after opening.

GINGER: Fresh ginger root is usually used in conjunction with garlic; do not use powdered ginger as a substitute. Scrape off the skin with a knife before using. Stored in a dark cupboard, ginger should keep for several weeks. See notes above on the use of crushed ginger.

JAGGERY: This is crude sugar, most commonly made from cane sugar and also from the sap of coconut or palmyrah palms. Southeast Asian palm sugar makes an acceptable substitute, or use soft brown sugar.

MACE: This lacy orangey red covering or aril of the nutmeg seed is used in some recipes for *garam masala*, especially in Muslim dishes. Mace is sold in powdered form, but it is preferable to grind your own blades of mace in an electric grinder.

DRIED MANGO POWDER: Unripe mangoes are dried and ground to make a powder (*amchoor*) which is used to give a sour tang to some dishes. If it is not available, a squeeze of lemon juice makes an acceptable substitute.

MINT: Widely used as a herb, the mint found in India is similar to that which grows elsewhere.

MUSTARD OIL: Oil made from ground mustards seeds is used as a cooking medium in some parts of India, particularly in Bengal. The flavour gives a distinctive difference to the food and is worth looking for in Indian stores; if mustard oil is not available, substitute any refined, flavourless vegetable oil.

MUSTARD SEEDS: Both yellow and brownish-black mustard seeds are used in Indian cuisine, the latter being more common in the south. Be sure to use the type specified.

NIGELLA: Often referred to as onion seeds, these small black seeds are known as *kalonjii* in India. Omit if not available; or if specified for Indian breads, substitute with black sesame seeds.

NUTMEG: Like cloves, this spice is a native of the Moluccan islands of Indonesia. The nutmeg is actually the seed of a fleshy fruit, and is covered by a lacy red membrane known as mace. Whole nutmeg should always be freshly grated just before using.

PAPADS: Also known as *poppadum*, these are wafer-thin discs of seasoned wheat and lentil flour which swell up and become deliciously crisp after frying for a few seconds in hot oil. Make sure they are thoroughly dry before frying. Served as an accompaniment to meals.

PEPPER: Peppercorns, from a vine thought to be native to the Malabar coast of India, are generally sold black (that is, with their skin intact) and are frequently added whole to dishes.

POPPY SEEDS: Tiny white poppy seeds are prized for their delicate nutty flavour and are also used as a thickening agent; they are generally soaked in warm water for 10–15 minutes and then ground before use. Substitute cashew nuts or almonds.

SAFFRON: The world's most expensive spice is actually the dried stigma of a type of crocus that grows in Kashmir (as well as in the Mediterranean and Turkey). The dried strands should be allowed to infuse in warm milk before being added to rice and dessert dishes. Store saffron in the deep-freeze as it loses its fragrance quickly, and never buy powdered saffron if you want the true aroma of this spice.

STAR ANISE: Coastal Indian communities with a long history of trade with the Far East use this Chinese spice in some dishes. Each star anise, which has a marked aniseed flavour, has eight hard brown petals with a shiny black seed inside. Use the entire spice.

TAMARIND: The pulp of tamarind pods, which grow on a large tree, is dried and used to add a fruity sourness to many dishes, particularly in southern India. Tamarind pulp, which keeps indefinitely on the shelf, should be soaked in warm water for about 5 minutes, then squeezed through a sieve and any fibres, skin and seeds discarded. Sometimes, the dried pulp is used directly without this preliminary soaking; be sure to pick it over carefully first and discard all fibrous material and stones.

TURMERIC: A ginger-like rhizome which is used fresh in Southeast Asian cooking, turmeric is always dried in India and sold as dried roots or in powdered form. As this bright yellow spice is very frequently adulterated with rice flour, you may find that the amounts specified in the recipes seem insufficient. Adjust according to taste, but beware of overdoing it as turmeric is quite pungent.

Nigella

Papad

Star Anise

Turmeric

Part Three: The Recipes

Basic recipes for pickles, chutneys, spice mixtures and milk products precede those for the main dishes, which begin on page 42

PICKLES AND RELISHES

Sabzi Achar
Mixed Vegetable Pickle

250 g (8 oz) each of carrots, unripe green mangoes, green chillies and lotus root
4 lemons, quartered
1 cup mustard oil
2 teaspoons fennel seeds
1 teaspoon nigella seeds
1 teaspoon black mustard seeds
$2^1/_2$ teaspoons chilli powder
$2^1/_2$ teaspoons turmeric powder
2 teaspoons *garam masala* (page 39)
1 onion, chopped and puréed
$1^1/_2$ tablepoons crushed ginger
$1^1/_2$ tablepoons crushed garlic
2 pinches of sodium benzoate
$^1/_2$ teaspoon acetic acid crystals
$4^1/_2$ tablespoons salt

Peel and cut the carrots and mango into small wedges. Peel and slice the lotus root. Leave the chillies whole. Heat the mustard oil to smoking point, then add the fennel, nigella and mustard seeds and sauté until the spices crackle. Add chilli powder, turmeric, *garam masala*, onion, ginger and garlic and stir, then add the vegetables and lemons. Take off the heat and add sodium benzoate, acetic acid

Measurements

Measurements in this book are given in volume as far as possible: 1 measuring **cup** contains 250 ml (roughly 8 oz); 1 **teaspoon** contains 5 ml, while 1 **tablespoon** contains 15 ml or the equivalent of 3 teaspoons. Australian readers please note that the standard Australian measuring spoon is larger, containing 20 ml or 4 teaspoons, so use only $^3/_4$ tablespoon when following the recipes. Where metric measurements are given, approximate imperial conversions follow in brackets.

Time Estimates

Time estimates, which assume the use of a blender or food processor for grinding, are for preparation only and do not include actual cooking time.

⏱ *quick and very easy to prepare*

⏱⏱ *relatively easy; less than 15 minutes' preparation*

⏱⏱⏱ *takes over 15 minutes to prepare*

Opposite:
Clockwise, from the top left: Lemon Mango Pickle (recipe page 36), chilli pickle (no recipe), Onion Mustard Pickle (page 36), green chilli pickle (no recipe) and Mixed Vegetable Pickle (this page).

and salt. Stir to mix well. Put the pickle in sterilised jars, making sure it is covered with oil. If necessary, add more oil which has first been heated to smoking point, then cooled. Keeps 3-4 months.

Pyaz Ka Achar
Onion Mustard Pickle

1 cup mustard oil
4 tablespoons black mustard seeds
2 teaspoons chilli powder
1 teaspoon turmeric powder
3 tablespoons vinegar
2$\frac{1}{2}$ tablespoons sugar
$\frac{1}{2}$ tablespoon salt
3 tablespoons dried mango powder
15–18 green chillies
30 cloves garlic, peeled and left whole
1$\frac{1}{2}$ tablespoons crushed ginger
1$\frac{1}{2}$ tablespoons crushed garlic
1 kg (2 lb) onions, sliced
$\frac{1}{2}$ teaspoon glacial acetic acid
pinch of sodium benzoate

Heat oil to smoking point, then set aside to cool. Grind or blend the mustard seeds, chilli, turmeric, vinegar, sugar, salt and mango powder to make a paste. Add this to the oil, together with all other ingredients. Stir to mix well and store in sterilised jars, with the pickle covered by oil. Keeps 3–4 weeks.

Nimbu Aur Aam Ka Achar
Lemon Mango Pickle

1 kg (2 lb) lemons, quartered
10–15 green chillies, halved lengthwise
3–4 unripe green mangoes, peeled and diced
1 cup lemon juice
1$\frac{1}{2}$ tablespoons cumin powder

1 tablespoon turmeric powder
1$\frac{1}{2}$ teaspoons chilli powder
4$\frac{1}{2}$ tablespoons salt
2$\frac{1}{2}$ tablespoons sugar
1$\frac{1}{2}$ cup mustard oil

Combine the lemons, chillies, mangoes and lemon juice in a bowl and sprinkle with the spices, salt and sugar. Put into a large glass jar covered loosely with a cloth and leave in the sun for 6 days. Heat the oil to smoking point, allow to cool and then stir into the lemon mixture. Leave in the sun for another 4 days, then cover the jar with a lid and store in a cool, dry place away from the light. Keeps for several months.

Saunth Ki Chatni
Tamarind & Ginger Chutney

100 g (3$\frac{1}{2}$ oz) dried tamarind pulp
5 dates, stones removed (optional)
1 teaspoon chilli powder
$\frac{3}{4}$ teaspoon ginger powder
$\frac{1}{4}$ teaspoon nigella seeds, toasted and ground
$\frac{3}{4}$ teaspoon fennel seeds, toasted and ground
1 teaspoon cumin seeds, toasted and ground
60 g (2 oz) palm sugar (*jaggery*)
1 teaspoon white sugar or more to taste
salt to taste

Soak the tamarind pulp with 2 cups of water for a minimum of 4 hours. Put pulp and liquid together with dates (if using) into a non-reactive pan, cover and simmer for 30 minutes. Push through a sieve, discarding the seeds and fibrous matter.

Return the sieved pulp to the pan and add chilli powder, ginger, nigella, fennel and cumin. Cook over low heat for 10 minutes, then add palm sugar and stir until dissolved. Add white sugar and salt to taste. Serve with any appetisers such as *Pakora* or *Samosa*, or serve with simple vegetable dishes for extra tang. Will keep refrigerated for about 1 week.

Hussaini Tamatar Qoot

Tomato Chutney

1 tablespoon oil
$^3/_4$ teaspoon black mustard seeds
$^1/_2$ teaspoon nigella seeds
1 sprig of curry leaves
pinch of asafoetida powder
4 green chillies, slit lengthwise and de-seeded
1 teaspoon crushed garlic
$^3/_4$ teaspoon crushed ginger
4 medium-sized ripe tomatoes, chopped
    coarsely
$^1/_2$ teaspoon turmeric powder
1 teaspoon chilli powder
2 teaspoons sugar
salt to taste

Heat oil and fry mustard seeds, nigella seeds, curry leaves and asafoetida until the spices start to crackle. Add the garlic and ginger and sauté gently for a couple of minutes, then put in the tomatoes and cook for about 10 minutes until the tomatoes turn pulpy. Add the turmeric, chilli powder and sugar and stir until the sugar dissolves. Add salt to taste and serve hot. This chutney keeps for 3–4 days if refrigerated in a covered jar.

Thenga Chatni

Coconut Chutney

250 g (8 oz) freshly grated coconut
3 green chillies, chopped
4–5 cloves garlic, chopped
1 cm ($^1/_2$ in) ginger, chopped
3 tablespoons split Bengal gram (*channa dal*)
$^1/_2$ teaspoon salt

Seasoning:

1 teaspoon oil
$^1/_4$ teaspoon black mustard seeds
$^1/_2$ teaspoon husked blackgram *dal* (*urad dal*)
1–2 dried chillies, broken and de-seeded
$^1/_2$ sprig curry leaves
pinch of asafoetida powder

Below:
Clockwise from top left: mango chutney (no recipe), Tomato Chutney (this page) and Tamarind and Ginger Chutney (page 36).

Blend the coconut with all other ingredients (except seasoning) in a food processor until coarse. Heat the oil and sauté the **seasoning** ingredients (except for asafoetida) until the mustard seeds start to pop. Add the asafoetida, stir, then take off the heat and mix in the coconut. Put into a bowl and serve with *Dosay, Idli, Vaday* or other southern Indian breads or snacks. **Green coconut chutney** can be made by adding 1 cup of mint leaves and ½ cup coriander leaves to the coconut.

Pudina Ki Chatni
Mint & Coriander Chutney

1 cup coriander leaves
½ cup mint leaves
2 green chillies, chopped
1 cm (½ in) ginger, chopped
3 cloves garlic, chopped
2 tablespoons plain yogurt
1 teaspoon sugar
½ teaspoon chilli powder
salt to taste
1 teaspoon *chaat masala* (page 39)
lemon juice to taste

Put all ingredients in a blender and process until very fine. Serve with snacks or *tandoori* dishes.

Mangga Thuvial
Green Mango Chutney

3 unripe green mangoes, weighing a total of about 500 g (1 lb)
½ teaspoon sesame seeds
3–4 dried chillies, broken in 2.5 cm (1 in) lengths
2 medium-sized onions, chopped

2 tablespoons freshly grated or desiccated coconut
1 sprig curry leaves
1 tablespoon chopped coriander leaves
1 teaspoon oil
1 teaspoon black mustard seeds
1½ teaspoons split Bengal gram (*channa dal*)
salt to taste

Peel the mangoes, discard the seeds and chop the flesh coarsely. Gently sauté the sesame seeds and chillies until crisp. Combine the mango flesh, sesame seeds, chillies, onion, coconut, curry leaves and coriander leaves and grind or blend coarsely. Heat the oil and fry mustard seeds and *dal* until the mustard seeds start to pop. Pour into the other ingredients, mix and add salt to taste and serve.

Mole de Camarao
Goan Prawn Pickle

½ cup oil
500 g (1 lb) medium-sized prawns, peeled and patted dry
½ teaspoon cumin seeds
¼ teaspoon black peppercorns
1 teaspoon turmeric powder
1 medium-sized onion, chopped
2–3 cloves garlic, chopped
2.5 cm (1 in) ginger, chopped
4 green cardamom pods, husks discarded
10 dried chillies, lightly fried until crisp
1 teaspoon cinnamon powder
1–2 cups vinegar
1 teaspoon salt

Heat oil and sauté the prawns for about 5 minutes, then drain and set aside. Grind or blend all other seasonings with just enough vinegar to make a paste. Dilute to a thin sauce with additional vinegar and simmer over low heat for $^1/_2$ hour. Add salt and cool.

Pack prawns into a sterilised glass jar and pour in sauce to cover. Make sure there is a layer of oil over the top of the prawns. Wait 3 days and enjoy. This pickle, an ideal accompaniment to seafood dishes, can be kept in the fridge for 1–2 months.

SPICE MIXTURES

Garam Masala

$^1/_2$ cup cumin seeds
2 tablespoons coriander seeds
4 cinnamon sticks, each 5 cm (2 in) long
10–12 green cardamom pods, bruised
4–5 black cardamom pods, bruised
10 cloves
$^1/_2$ nutmeg, broken
3–4 blades of mace
1 tablespoon black peppercorns
4 whole star anise
5 bay leaves

Put all the spices in a dry pan (preferably non stick) and heat over a very low fire, shaking the pan from time to time. When the spices give off a fragrance, allow to cool slightly, then grind finely in a coffee mill or electric blender. Store in an airtight bottle. (If stored in the deep-freeze portion of the fridge, spices keep fresh almost indefinitely.)

Rasam Masala

2 teaspoons coriander seeds
$^1/_2$ teaspoon cumin seeds
1 teaspoon fenugreek seeds
1 teaspoon black peppercorns
1 teaspoon black mustard seeds
6 dried chillies, broken into several pieces
1 sprig curry leaves
$^1/_2$ teaspoon husked blackgram *dal* (*urad dal*)
$^1/_2$ teaspoon split Bengal gram (*channa dal*)
pinch of asafoetida powder

Put all ingredients except asafoetida in a pan over low heat and cook until the chillies become crisp and the spices smell fragrant, taking care not to burn them. Cool slightly, then grind all ingredients together, then mix with the asafoetida powder. This is used to flavour the southern Indian soup, *Rasam*.

Kadai Masala

6 dried chillies, broken into several pieces
2 tablespoons coriander seeds
$^1/_4$ teaspoon *garam masala*

Heat chillies and coriander in a pan, shaking from time to time, until they smell fragrant. Grind and add *garam masala*.

Chaat Masala

1 tablespoon cumin seeds
1 tablespoon black peppercorns
5 cloves
3 cubeb or long pepper (optional)
$^1/_2$ tablespoon dried mint leaves
$^1/_4$ teaspoon carom seeds (*ajwain*)
$^1/_4$ teaspoon asafoetida powder
1 tablespoon rock salt
$2^1/_2$ tablespoons dried mango powder
1 teaspoon ginger powder
1 teaspoon chilli powder

$^1/_4$ teaspoon tartaric acid
2 teaspoons refined salt

Put first seven ingredients in a dry pan and heat gently, shaking the pan from time to time, until the spices begin to smell fragrant. Remove from heat, add the rock salt and grind while still warm. Mix in all other ingredients, cool and store tightly bottled. This salty, sour *chaat masala* (the approximate translation of the name is "finger licking"!) is sprinkled over cooked food for additional flavour.

DRINKS

Thandai
Rich Milk Drink

1 litre (4 cups) fresh milk
3 tablespoons unsalted melon seeds
2 tablespoons blanched almonds
2 tablespoons raw cashew nuts
$1^1/_2$ tablespoons white poppy seeds, soaked and
    simmered 15 minutes
$1^1/_2$ teaspoons black peppercorns
1 teaspoon fennel seeds
large pinch of saffron
5 green cardamom pods, bruised
petals from 1 red rose, or few drops of rose
    essence
5–6 tablespoons sugar
1 heaped tablespoon skinned, unsalted
    pistachio nuts, finely chopped

Put 1 cup of the milk together with all other ingredients, except the pistachios, and blend to make a paste. Push through a sieve lined with muslin or cheesecloth. Add remaining milk to the sieved mixture and check for sweetness. Chill for 3–4 hours

to blend the flavours and serve in glasses, each garnished with a little chopped pistachio.

Jal Jeera
Savoury Cumin Drink

2 tablespoons black cumin seeds
2 teaspoons dried mango powder
1 teaspoon ginger powder
$^1/_2$ teaspoon black peppercorns
$1^1/_2$ teaspoons dried mint
$^1/_2$ teaspoon chilli powder
$^1/_4$ teaspoon carom seeds (*ajwain*)
$^1/_4$ teaspoon asafoetida powder
4 cloves
$1^1/_2$ teaspoons rock salt
1 teaspoon refined salt

Combine all ingredients in a dry pan and toast until they smell fragrant. Cool slightly, then blend to a powder. Keep in a tightly covered jar. When the drink is required, use 1 teaspoon of this powder to 1 glass of water. Add 1 teaspoon of mint & coriander chutney (page 38) and $^1/_4$ teaspoon sugar per glass and garnish with mint leaves.

MISCELLANEOUS

Kachumber
Onion, Tomato & Cucumber Relish

1 medium-sized onion, finely diced
2 medium-sized tomatoes, finely diced
10 cm (4 in) piece cucumber, finely diced
1 tablespoon chopped coriander leaves
1 green chilli, de-seeded and chopped
$^1/_4$ teaspoon chilli powder
$^1/_2$ teaspoon salt
juice of 2 lemons

Mix onions, tomatoes and cucumber with coriander, green chilli and chilli powder. Immediately before serving, mix with salt and lemon juice and serve as with *Dhansak Dal* or any other main meal dish.

Dahi
Plain Yogurt

4 cups (1 litre) fresh milk
2 tablespoons full-cream powdered milk
1 tablespoon plain yogurt

Combine the fresh and powdered milks, stirring to dissolve, then put over moderate heat and bring almost to the boil, stirring from time to time. Remove from the heat and allow to cool to a little over blood heat. You should be able to hold your finger in the milk up to the count of 10 without it stinging. Put the plain yogurt starter in a clean container and stir in the hot milk. Cover with a cloth and leave in a warm place until set. In cooler temperatures, a wide-mouth insulated jar or thermos flask should ensure that the temperature stays warm enough for the yogurt to set. Refrigerate the yogurt as soon as it has set and use some of this as a starter for your next batch.

Before it is used in Indian cuisine, yogurt is often vigorously stirred to ensure the whey is reincorporated with the curds; this is referred to as **whipped yogurt**. Yogurt that is drained for several hours to remove the whey is called **hung yogurt** (see page 29 for advice on how to make this).

Chenna/Paneer
Home-made Cream Cheese

4 cups (1 litre) fresh milk
1 tablespoon vinegar mixed with 1 tablespoon water or 2 tablespoons plain yogurt
2 cups cold water

Put the milk into a heavy bottomed pan and bring slowly to the boil, stirring occasionally. Remove from heat and let the milk cool down so that it is still hot, but not burning to the touch (75°C/167°F). Add the vinegar and water or yogurt, stirring vigorously until the milk starts to curdle. Immediately add the water to reduce the temperature and prevent the mixture becoming tough. Strain through a muslin or cheesecloth-lined sieve until all the whey has drained off. The curds left are known as **chenna** and should be kneaded lightly to make a smooth mixture, then refrigerated until needed for various desserts. To obtain **paneer**, wrap the cheese in the same cheesecloth and shape into an oblong or square. Wrap tightly and place it under a heavy weight for about 2 hours to compress it. Remove the weight and cut into desired shapes.

Khoa
Condensed Milk

4 cups (1 litre) fresh milk

Bring the milk to the boil in a wide, heavy-bottomed pan, stirring constantly. Continue stirring over high heat until the milk dries into a lump, which will take about 25 minutes; this will make about 90 g (3 oz) *khoa*.

SAMOSA & KELE KA TIKKA

Vegetable-stuffed Pastries & Deep-fried Plantain and Potato Balls

VEGETABLE-STUFFED PASTRIES
⏱ ⏱ ⏱

100 g ($3^1/_2$ oz) *ghee* or butter
250 g (8 oz) plain flour
$^1/_2$ teaspoon carom seeds (*ajwain*)
$^1/_2$ teaspoon salt
water to make a firm dough
oil for deep frying

Filling:

3 tablespoons oil
$^1/_2$ teaspoon cumin seeds
250 g (8 oz) potato, boiled and finely diced
50 g ($1^1/_2$ oz) green peas, cooked
$^1/_2$ teaspoon salt
1 teaspoon coriander powder
$^1/_2$ teaspoon turmeric powder
$^1/_2$-1 teaspoon chilli powder
1 green chilli, de-seeded and finely chopped
1 teaspoon dried mango powder

Opposite:
*Vegetable-stuffed
Pastries (left),
Potato & Plantain
Balls (centre) and
Batter-coated
Vegetables (right),
shown with Mint
Chutney (page
38). Recipe for
Batter-coated
Vegetables is on
page 44.*

Rub *ghee* or butter into the flour until the mixture is crumbly. Mix in the carom seeds and salt, then add sufficient water to make a firm but pliable dough. Leave for 30 minutes, covered with a damp cloth.

Prepare the **filling**. Sauté the cumin seeds until they crackle, add remaining ingredients and sauté or 1 minute. Leave to cool. Roll out the pastry thinly, then cut into circles 8 cm (3 in) in diameter. Cut each circle in half. Put a spoonful of filling on one semi-circle of pastry and roll over the top, pressing the edges firmly to seal. Heat oil and deep fry the *samosa*s until golden brown.

PLANTAIN & POTATO BALLS ⏱ ⏱

350 g ($11^1/_2$ oz) plantains, steamed until soft
150 g (5 oz) boiled potatoes, mashed
1 teaspoon *chaat masala* (page 39)
1 teaspoon coriander seeds, toasted and ground
$^1/_4$ teaspoon *garam masala*
$^1/_2$ teaspoon salt
2 cm ($^3/_4$ in) ginger, finely chopped
1 heaped tablespoon chopped coriander leaf
2 green chillies, de-seeded and finely chopped
1 heaped tablespoon cornflour
100 g ($3^1/_2$ oz) fine wheat vermicelli, broken
    into small pieces
oil for deep frying

Grate the steamed plantains, then combine with the potato and all other ingredients except vermicelli and oil. Mix well, then shape into balls and roll in the vermicelli, pressing to make sure the vermicelli adheres. Heat oil and deep fry the balls until golden brown.

Helpful hints: If plantains are not available, use 500g/1lb potatoes.

MADDHU VADAY & PAKORA
Fried Savoury Dumplings & Batter-coated Vegetables

FRIED SAVOURY DUMPLINGS ☺☺☺

500 g (1 lb) rice
250 g (8 oz) husked blackgram *dal* (*urad da*l)
4 tablespoons plain yogurt
2¹/₂ tablespoons oil
1 teaspoon baking powder
1 teaspoon salt
1 tablespoon oil
1 teaspoon black mustard seeds
1 tablespoon split Bengal gram (*channa dal*)
2-3 dried chillies, broken in 2.5 cm (1 in)
  lengths
8-10 raw cashew nuts, broken
1 sprig curry leaves
oil for deep frying

Opposite:
*Fried Savoury
Dumplings (right)
with a selection of
fresh chutneys
and Idli
(no recipe).
Photograph of
Batter-coated
Vegetables is on
page 43.*

Soak 400 g (12¹/₂ oz) of the rice and all the *dal* overnight. Soak the remaining 100 g (3¹/₂ oz) rice for just 30 minutes, then drain and spread on a cloth to dry for about 1¹/₂ hours. Grind in a food processor until coarse.

Grind the rice soaked overnight, adding just enough water to make a stiff paste. Set aside and grind the *dal* in a similar fashion. Combine both lots of rice and *dal,* yogurt, 2¹/₂ tablespoons oil, baking powder and salt.

Heat 1 tablespoon oil and fry the mustard seeds, Bengal gram, dried chillies, cashews and curry leaves until the mustard seeds start to pop, then add to the dough. Shape the dough like doughnuts and deep fry in hot oil for about 5 minutes, until cooked through and golden brown.

BATTER-COATED VEGETABLES ☺☺

1 potato, peeled
1 small aubergine (eggplant)
1 large onion
2 cups Bengal gram flour (*besan*)
1 teaspoon salt
1 teaspoon chilli powder
¹/₂ teaspoon bicarbonate of soda
water

Cut the potato in half lengthwise, then cut in slices about 0.5 cm (¹/₄ in) thick. Do not peel the aubergine but cut in slices the same size as the potato. Peel the onion and slice the same thickness. Set the vegetables aside.

Combine flour, salt, chilli powder and salt, mixing well. Add enough cold water to make a very thick batter of coating consistency.

Heat oil and dip the vegetables, one at a time, into the batter, coating thoroughly. Deep fry until half-cooked (about 2-3 minutes), then drain and set aside. Just before the *pakora* are needed, re-heat the oil and deep fry until golden brown and cooked through. Serve hot.

CHICKEN MASALA & LIVER ON TOAST

CHICKEN MASALA ON TOAST

These two Ango-Indian dishes are very mildly spiced and served, British-style, on hot toast. 🕐🕐

500 g (1 lb) boneless chicken, diced
$^1/_2$ cup hung yogurt (page 41)
1 teaspoon chilli paste
$^1/_2$ teaspoon *garam masala* (page 39)
$^1/_2$ teaspoon crushed garlic
$^1/_2$ teaspoon crushed ginger
juice of 1 lemon
$1^1/_2$ tablespoons oil or butter
2 medium onions, sliced
$^1/_4$ teaspoon coriander powder
$^1/_4$ teaspoon chilli powder
salt and pepper to taste
4 tomatoes, chopped
2 tablespoons finely choped coriander leaves

Opposite:
*Chicken Masala
on Toast (top of
plate) and
Chicken Liver on
Toast (bottom).*

Marinate the chicken in yogurt, chilli paste, *garam masala*, $^1/_4$ teaspoon each of the garlic and ginger and the lemon juice for 30 minutes.

Heat oil in a heavy pan and sauté the onions until light brown. Add the spices and remaining garlic and ginger and sauté until they smell fragrant. Add the chicken together with the marinade, stir for a minute, then put in the tomatoes and simmer,

uncovered, until the chicken is tender. Remove the chicken and keep cooking the sauce until it has thickened. Remove sauce from heat, stir in the coriander and the chicken. Serve warm spread on hot buttered toast.

CHICKEN LIVER ON TOAST 🕐🕐

1 tablespoon oil
2 medium-sized onions, sliced
1 cup chicken livers, cleaned
$^1/_4$ teaspoon chilli powder
$^1/_4$ teaspoon coriander powder
$^1/_4$ teaspoon *garam masala* (page 39)
$^1/_2$ teaspoon crushed ginger
1 medium-sized tomato, chopped
salt and pepper to taste
1 tablespoon finely chopped coriander leaves

Heat oil and sauté onions until transparent, then add chicken livers and sauté until they just start to change colour. Add the spices and ginger, sauté for 2 minutes, then put in the tomatoes and cook over high heat until the livers are cooked and the sauce reduced. Add salt and pepper and the chopped coriander and serve warm spread on hot buttered toast.

Relief !!!

Oh, to be playing on Grass Courts — at home!

RAAB & NIMMA RASAM
Yogurt Soup & Spiced Lentil Soup

YOGURT SOUP

Rajasthani cooks often reserve the fragrant oil (*rogan*) that rises to the top of any meat curry and use this as a garnish, as in this yogurt soup. ☉☉

1 tablespoon oil
$^1/_2$ teaspoon black mustard seeds
2 green chillies, chopped
$^1/_2$ teaspoon crushed garlic
$^1/_4$ teaspoon crushed ginger
$^3/_4$ cup plain yogurt
3 cups water or chicken or vegetable stock
salt to taste
a pinch of turmeric powder
a pinch of chilli powder
1 teaspoon finely chopped coriander leaves
$^1/_2$ teaspoon finely chopped mint leaves
1 teaspoon fragrant oil for garnish (optional)

Heat oil in a large pan and add the mustard seeds. As soon as they crackle, add green chillies, garlic and ginger. Sauté for 5 minutes, then add the yogurt, water and salt to taste.

Simmer over low heat for 10-15 minutes, stirring constantly to prevent the yogurt from curdling. Add the turmeric and chilli powder, coriander and mint leaves, mix well and serve hot garnished with the fragrant oil.

SPICED LENTIL SOUP ☉☉

75 g (2$^1/_2$ oz) yellow *dal* (*tuvar dal*)
4 cups water
1$^1/_2$ tablespoons oil
1 teaspoon black mustard seeds
3 cloves garlic, crushed
1 sprig curry leaves
1-2 dried chillies, broken in 2.5 cm (1 in) pieces
6-8 whole black peppercorns, coarsely crushed
a pinch of turmeric powder
a pinch of asafoetida powder
1 medium-sized ripe tomato, quartered
salt to taste
1 teaspoon *rasam masala* (page 39)
juice of 2 lemons
1 teaspoon finely chopped coriander leaves

Wash the *dal* and simmer with water until the *dal* disintegrates. Sieve the *dal* and its liquid into a pan and keep warm.

Heat oil, add the mustard seeds and when they start to crackle, add the garlic, curry leaves, chillies, pepper, turmeric and asafoetida. Sauté for a few seconds then pour onto the *dal*. Add tomato, salt, *rasam masala* and lemon juice. Simmer for a couple of minutes and serve hot, garnished with the coriander leaves.

MOOLOOGOO THANI

Mulligatawny Soup

The inspiration for this Anglo-Indian soup was southern Indian "pepper water", which certainly did not include apple, curry powder and chicken. This flavourful soup is still a favourite among the Westernised middle-class, who enjoy it in their private clubs. ☻☻

2 tablespoons oil
1 teaspoon crushed ginger
1 teaspoon crushed garlic
1 large onion, sliced
2 tablespoons Bengal gram flour (*besan*)
1 green apple, peeled and diced
1 heaped tablespoon curry powder
$1/4$ teaspoon turmeric powder
2 medium-sized tomatoes
1 bay leaf
1 teaspoon coarsely ground black pepper
3 cups chicken stock
1-2 tablespoons boiled rice (optional)
100 g ($3^1/_2$ oz) cooked chicken, shredded
lemon wedges

Heat the oil and add the ginger and garlic. Sauté for 2 minutes, then add the onion and sauté until the onion is transparent.

Add the gram flour, apple, curry powder, turmeric, tomatoes, bay leaf, pepper and chicken stock. Bring to the boil, cover and reduce heat. Simmer for 45 minutes, then process in a blender or pass through a sieve. Add the rice (if using) and chicken, stir well and serve with lemon wedges.

CHAPATI & PURI
Unleavened Bread & Deep-fried Bread

UNLEAVENED BREAD

For the best result, *chapati* should be properly kneaded; using slow speed and a plastic blade in a food processor is an acceptable alternative to 10-15 minutes of hand-kneading. ◒ ◔

2 cups fine wholemeal flour (*atta*)
about $1/2$ cup warm water
2 teaspoons softened *ghee* or butter

Mix the flour and water in a bowl to make a dough that is pliable yet not too sticky. Add *ghee* or butter and turn the mixture out onto a floured board or put in a food processor. Knead by hand for 10-15 minutes or process at low speed for 5 minutes. Roll into a ball, cover with a damp cloth and set aside for at least 1 hour.

Knead the dough again for 3-4 minutes, then break into pieces the size of a golf ball. Flatten into a circle with your hands, then roll out into circles about 20 cm (8 in) in diameter.

Heat a heavy griddle (*tawa*) or frying pan until very hot. Put on a *chapati* and cook until brown spots appear underneath. Turn over and cook the other side, pressing on the top of the *chapati* with a clean cloth to help make air bubbles form and keep the *chapati* light. As each *chapati* is cooked, wrap in a clean cloth to keep warm. Serve with curries, *dal* or vegetables.

DEEP-FRIED BREAD

Puri are a delicious alternative to *chapati* and use exactly the same dough. To ensure they puff up when cooking, keep flicking the oil over the top while the *puri* are frying. ◒ ◔

1 quantity of *chapati* dough
oil for deep frying

Roll out the dough as for *chapati*, make into 20 cm (8 in) circles and cover with a cloth. Heat plenty of oil in a wok until very hot. Put in a *puri* and immediately start flicking hot oil over the top of it with a spatula so that it will swell up like a ball. This should take only a few seconds. Flip the *puri* over and cook on the other side until golden brown. Serve immediately with curries, *dal* or vegetables.

Opposite:
Deep-fried Bread (left) and Unleavened Bread (right).

NAAN & LUCCHI
Tandoor-baked Bread & Bengali Fried Bread

TANDOOR-BAKED BREAD

This bread gets its characteristic tear-drop shape from the way the dough droops as it cooks on the wall of a *tandoor*. ⏱ ⏱

500 g (1 lb) plain flour
$^{1}/_{2}$ teaspoon baking powder
1 teaspoon salt
$^{1}/_{2}$ cup milk
1 tablespoon sugar
1 egg
4 tablespoons oil
1 teaspoon nigella seeds

Sift the flour, baking powder and salt together into a bowl and make a well in the middle. Mix the milk, sugar, egg and 2 tablespoons of the oil in a bowl. Pour this into the centre of the flour and knead, adding more water if necessary to form a soft dough. Add the remaining oil, knead again, then cover with a damp cloth and allow the dough to stand for 15 minutes.

Knead the dough again, cover and leave for 2-3 hours. About half an hour before the *naan* are required, turn on the oven to the maximum heat. Divide the dough into 8 balls and let them rest for 3-5 minutes. Sprinkle a baking sheet with the nigella seeds and put it in to oven to heat up while the dough is resting. Shape each ball of dough with the palms to make an oval shape. Bake the *naan* until puffed up and golden brown. Serve hot.

BENGALI FRIED BREAD

Lucchi are similar to *puri*, except for the addition of semolina for texture and fennel for fragrance. ⏱ ⏱

1 cup plain flour
$^{1}/_{2}$ teaspoon salt
1 tablespoon fine semolina
1 teaspoon fennel seeds, lightly toasted and
**   ground**
1 tablespoon oil
$^{1}/_{4}$ cup water
***ghee* or oil for deep frying**

Sieve flour and salt into a large bowl, then add semolina and fennel, mixing well. Combine oil and water, then mix in with the dry ingredients and knead well to make a smooth dough, adding more water if necessary. Cover bowl with a cloth and set dough aside for 15 minutes.

Divide the dough into 8 balls, flatten each with the palm of your hand, then roll out to make disks of 10-12 cm (4-5 in). Heat *ghee* or oil in a wok until very hot, then deep fry the bread, one at a time, flicking the hot *ghee* or oil over the top so that it puffs up. Turn and cook on the other side until golden.

APPAM & VECCHU PARATHA

Rice-flour Pancakes & Flaky Fried Bread

RICE-FLOUR PANCAKES ☻☻☻

3 cups rice, soaked in water for 6 hours or
  overnight
1 cup husked blackgram *dal* (*urad dal*), soaked
  for 4 hours
$^1/_4$ cup plain yogurt
2 teaspoons dried yeast, soaked in $^1/_4$ cup warm
  water
$^1/_4$ cup coconut milk or more
1 teaspoon salt
oil to grease the pan

Opposite: Rice-flour Pancakes (left) and Flaky Fried Bread (right).

Drain the soaked rice and *dal*. Put rice in a food processor and grind until it forms a thick paste. Remove and put in a large bowl. Process the *dal* and then combine with the rice. Add yogurt and yeast and leave to ferment for several hours. Refrigerate the batter as soon as it has started to ferment.

Just before cooking the *appam*, check the consistency of the batter, adding as much coconut milk as necessary to make a batter slightly thicker than the normal pancake consistency.

Grease a small heavy wok and heat. Pour in a ladleful of the mixture. Grab both sides of the wok with your hands and swirl it to spread the batter to make circle. Cover with a lid and cook for 3-4 minutes on low flame. The edges of the *appam* should be brown and crispy and the centre thick and moist. Serve with coconut chutney.

FLAKY FRIED BREAD

These wonderfully light breads are normally flung out in circles, like a fisherman throwing his net (*vecchu*) until paper thin. They can be hand-pulled like strudel for a similar result. ☻☻

4 cups plain white flour, sifted
3 eggs, lightly beaten
1 cup water
1 teaspoon salt
$^3/_4$ cup oil

Make a very soft dough with flour, eggs, salt and water, kneading well. Divide into balls about 5 cm (2 in) in diameter, cover with a damp cloth and leave to stand for 30 minutes.

Spread out each ball on a well oiled table top, pulling the edge gently with the hands to stretch it out as wide and as thin as possible, as for a strudel. Dust the surface with flour and fold over and over in a pleat fashion. Roll up the pleated dough to make a curled ball and leave to rest for 15 minutes. Use your hands to pat the ball into circles about 15 cm (6 in) in diameter, or use a rolling pin.

Oil a griddle or heavy frying pan and cook the bread, turning so that it is golden brown on each side. Repeat until all the dough is used up. Serve hot with *dal* or curries.

DOSAY

Southern Indian Rice-flour Pancakes

A Southern Indian breakfast favourite, these tangy pancakes are often served with fresh coconut chutney and tomato chutney, with *dal* as a dip. Alternatively, they can be stuffed with spiced potato to make *Masala Dosay*. ☺ ☺ ☺

3 cups long-grain rice
1 cup husked blackgram dal (*urad dal*)
1 teaspoon salt
1 onion, cut in half
3 tablespoons oil

Put the rice and *dal* into separate bowls, cover each with water and soak overnight. Grind the rice and *dal* separately in a food processor, adding a little water if necessary to obtain a smooth consistency. Mix the ground rice and *dal* together and leave at room temperature for up to 24 hours to ferment. The dough can now be refrigerated for up to 24 hours until required.

Stir the dough, adding salt and sufficient water to achieve the consistency of a very thick cream. Heat a non-stick pan or heavy griddle and rub with half an onion. Grease lightly with a little of the oil and pour in a ladle (about $\frac{1}{4}$ cup) of the batter, smearing it quickly with the back of the ladle to form a thin pancake about 12-15 cm (5-6 in) in diameter. Cook for about 2 to 3 minutes until the bottom is golden and the top is starting to set. Turn over and cook on the other side, then serve hot with coconut chutney (page 37).

Helpful hints: If liked, stuff the *dosay* with hot spiced potato or, for a non-vegetarian treat, with boneless Chicken Masala.

CHITRANNAM & THENGAI SADAM
Lemon Rice & Coconut Rice

LEMON RICE ☼☼

1¹⁄₂ cups long-grain rice, washed and drained
1 tablespoon oil
1 teaspoon black mustard seeds
a pinch of asafoetida powder
1 sprig curry leaves
¹⁄₂ teaspoon finely chopped ginger
¹⁄₂ green chilli, finely chopped
3–4 dried chillies, broken in 2.5 cm (1 in)
   pieces
1 tablespoon split raw cashews, lightly toasted
1 teaspoon husked blackgram *dal* (*urad dal*)
1 teaspoon split Bengal gram (*channa dal*),
   lightly toasted
¹⁄₂ teaspoon turmeric powder
1¹⁄₂ tablespoons lemon juice
salt to taste
1 tablespoon water
coriander leaf to garnish

Opposite:
Lemon Rice (top left) and Coconut Rice (bottom right).

Boil the rice in plenty of water until the grains are just tender. Drain thoroughly and keep aside.

Heat oil in a pan and add the mustard seeds. When they begin to pop, add asafoetida, curry leaves, ginger, chillies, cashews, blackgram *dal*, Bengal gram and turmeric powder. Sauté for a few seconds, then add lemon juice, salt and water. Simmer for 2–3 minutes, then toss in the rice and heat through. Serve garnished with coriander leaves.

COCONUT RICE ☼☼

250 g (8 oz) Basmati rice, washed and drained
1 teaspoon black mustard seeds
3–5 dried chillies, broken in 2.5 cm (1 in)
   lengths
2 green chillies, sliced
1–2 cloves garlic, finely chopped
1 cm (¹⁄₂ in) ginger, finely chopped
3 tablespoons oil
1 teaspoon husked blackgram *dal* (*urad dal*)
2 tablespoons split Bengal gram (*channa dal*)
1 sprig curry leaves
pinch of turmeric
pinch of asafoetida powder
1 teaspoon salt
150 g (5 oz) freshly grated coconut, roasted
   until golden brown
fresh coriander leaves to garnish

Boil rice for just 5 minutes, drain well and spread out on a tray to cool. Sauté mustard seeds, chillies, garlic and ginger in oil until the seeds begin to pop. Add both lots of *dal*, curry leaves and turmeric and sauté until the *dal* turns golden. Add asafoetida, salt, coconut and rice and mix thoroughly.

Remove from the heat and set the rice aside for 1 hour to allow the flavours to penetrate. Re-heat and serve garnished with coriander and, if liked, a few shreds of fresh coconut.

SABZI PULAO & TUVAR DAL KHICHDEE
Vegetable Pulao & Rice and Lentils

VEGETABLE PULAO

An ideal dish for vegetarians, this *pulao* can also include additional vegetables such as diced potatoes, green peas or small pieces of cauliflower if liked. ⏱⏱

2 cups long-grain rice (preferably Basmati)
2 tablespoons *ghee* or butter
1 teaspoon cumin seeds
5 cm (2 in) cinnamon stick
2–3 green cardamom pods, bruised
4–5 cloves
1 medium onion, sliced
1 tablespoon yogurt
1 ripe tomato, chopped
30 g (1 oz) green beans, finely sliced
30 g (1 oz) carrot, finely diced
1 teaspoon salt
fresh coriander leaves to garnish

Opposite:
Rice and Lentils (left) and Vegetable Pulao (right), with yogurt.

Wash the rice and soak in water for 30 minutes. Heat *ghee* and sauté the cumin, cinnamon, cardamom and cloves until the spices begin to crackle. Add the onion and fry until golden, then put in the yogurt and vegetables. Add $\frac{1}{2}$ cup of water, cover and simmer for 5 minutes.

Add $3\frac{1}{2}$ cups water, the drained rice and salt. Stir and bring to the boil, then simmer uncovered until the water has been completely absorbed. Cover the pan with a damp towel, put on the lid and cook over very low heat for about 5–10 minutes. Take off the heat but do not remove the lid. Stand for 15–20 minutes, then stir the rice gently with a fork. Serve garnished with coriander.

RICE AND LENTILS

The inspiration for Anglo-Indian "kedgeree", this is a simple mixture of rice and lentils. ⏱

100 g (3$\frac{1}{2}$ oz) rice
50 g (1$\frac{1}{2}$ oz) *dal* (yellow *tuvar dal*, Bengal gram or green mung pea *dal*)
4 cups water
salt to taste
1 tablespoon oil
$\frac{1}{2}$ teaspoon cumin seeds
1–2 green chillies (optional)
a pinch of asafoetida powder
a pinch of turmeric powder

Clean and wash rice and *dal*. If using Bengal gram or *tuvar dal*, simmer in water until just soft, then drain. If using mung *dal*, there is no need for this preliminary step. Combine *dal* with rice, water and salt, cover and simmer until very soft.

Heat the oil, then fry the cumin seeds, chillies, asafoetida and turmeric until the spices begin to crackle. Pour over the top of the cooked rice and serve hot.

RAJMAH & DAL MAHARANI
Spicy Pinto Beans & Bean and Lentil Stew

SPICY PINTO BEANS ⏲⏲

200 g (7 oz) dried pinto or kidney beans
5 cups water
2–3 tablespoons oil
2 black cardamom pods, bruised
4 medium-sized onions, chopped
2 teaspoons crushed garlic
1 teaspoon crushed ginger
1 teaspoon chilli paste
1$\frac{1}{2}$ teaspoons coriander powder
1 teaspoon cumin powder
$\frac{1}{2}$ teaspoon turmeric powder
2–3 medium-sized tomatoes, chopped
2 green chillies, sliced
2 tablespoons chopped coriander leaves
salt to taste
$\frac{1}{4}$ teaspoon *garam masala*

Opposite:
*Bean and Lentil
Stew (top left)
with a Sambar
Dal (bottom right,
no recipe).
Photograph of
Spicy Pinto Beans
is on page 71.*

Simmer the beans in water until just tender. Drain, reserving 1 cup of the cooking liquid. Heat the oil and sauté the cardamoms and onions until golden. Add the garlic, ginger and chilli and sauté for about 5 minutes, until the oil separates. Add the coriander, cumin and turmeric powder and sauté for 2-3 minutes over very low heat. Add the tomatoes and cook for 2 minutes. Add the beans, reserved cooking liquid, chillies, half the coriander and salt. Simmer uncovered until the beans are soft. Add a pinch of *garam masala* and cook 5 minutes. Serve garnished with remaining coriander and *garam masala*.

BEAN AND LENTIL STEW ⏲⏲

100 g (3$\frac{1}{2}$ oz) whole blackgram *dal* (*urad dal*), with the skin still on
30 g (1 oz) dried pinto or kidney beans
2.5 cm (1 in) ginger, sliced
$\frac{1}{2}$ teaspoon salt
2 tablespoons *ghee* or butter
1 teaspoon cumin seeds
1-2 green chillies, slit lengthwise
2 medium-sized tomatoes, chopped
$\frac{1}{2}$ cup cream
1 teaspoon *garam masala*

Soak the blackgram *dal* overnight, then drain. Soak the pinto or kidney beans for 4 hours, then drain. Combine *dal* and beans in a pan with ginger, salt and water to cover. Bring to the boil, cover the pan and simmer until just soft.

Heat the *ghee* or butter, add cumin seeds and chillies and sauté until the cumin seeds crackle. Add to the cooked *dal* together with the tomatoes and simmer until the tomatoes soften. Keep aside 1 tablespoon of the cream for garnish and add the rest to the pan. Heat through and serve garnished with reserved cream and *garam masala*. Serve with Indian bread.

UNDIYA

Spiced Mixed Vegetables

This Gujarati dish, a combination of mixed vegetables seasoned with spices and fresh coconut, is served as part of a main meal. It goes well with any type of Indian bread or rice. If yam or plantains are unavailable, increase the amounts of potato, aubergine and sweet potato slightly. ⊘ ⊘

*Opposite:
Spiced Mixed
Vegetables (top
left) on a chapati,
and Stuffed
Home-made
Cheese (recipe
page 68) with
Flaky Fried
Bread (page 56).*

75 g (2¹/₂ oz) red *dal* (*masoor dal*), soaked 4
    hours in warm water
75 g (2¹/₂ oz) tomatoes, coarsely chopped
75 g (2¹/₂ oz) small new potatoes, or peeled
    diced potatoes
75 g (2¹/₂ oz) aubergine (eggplant), diced
75 g (2¹/₂ oz) sweet potatoes, peeled and diced
75 g (2¹/₂ oz) purple or white yam, peeled and
    diced (optional)
75 g (2¹/₂ oz) plantain, peeled and diced (op-
    tional)
2 tablespoons oil
1 teaspoon cumin seeds
¹/₂ teaspoon carom seeds (*ajwain*)
pinch of asafoetida powder
2 tablespoons freshly grated or moistened des-
    iccated coconut, to garnish

Masala:

2 tablespoons coriander seeds
1 teaspoon cumin seeds
¹/₂ teaspoon carom seeds (*ajwain*)
2 tablespoons raw peanuts

3–4 green chillies, chopped
2 tablespoons chopped coriander leaves
1 teaspoon crushed garlic
1 teaspoon crushed ginger
4 tablespoons freshly grated coconut or moist-
    ened desiccated coconut
2 tablespoons chopped palm sugar (*jaggery*)
¹/₂ teaspoon salt

Drain the soaked *dal*. Prepare all the vegetables and set aside. Prepare the **masala** by toasting the coriander, cumin, carom seeds and peanuts together until the spices crackle, then grind to a powder. Combine with all other *masala* ingredients and blend or process until fine.

Heat the oil in a pan and sauté the cumin, carom and asafoetida until the spices start to crackle. Add the ground *masala* and sauté for about 5 minutes. Put in the tomatoes and continue cooking until they soften, then add the drained *dal* and prepared vegetables. Cover the pan and cook gently until the vegetables are tender. Sprinkle with the garnish of coconut and serve.

PANEER TIKKA & PANEER SHASHLIK
Stuffed & Skewered Home-made Cheese

STUFFED HOME-MADE CHEESE ◷ ◷

These two dishes using *paneer* are vegetarian alternatives to popular meat or poultry recipes.

500 g (1 lb) *paneer* (page 41)
2-3 tablespoons mint chutney (page 38)
1 cup hung yogurt (page 41)
1¹/₂ teaspoons crushed garlic
1¹/₂ teaspoons crushed ginger
1 teaspoon turmeric powder
1 teaspoon white pepper powder
¹/₂ teaspoon *garam masala*
salt to taste
1¹/₂ tablespoons oil
1¹/₂ teaspoons lemon juice

Cut the *paneer* into slices about 2 cm (³/₄ in) thick and 5 cm (2 in) square. Cut a small pocket into one side of each *paneer* and stuff with about ¹/₄ teaspoon of mint chutney.

Mix all remaining ingredients together to make a marinade and rub this onto the pieces of *paneer*. Leave to marinate for 45-60 minutes. Skewer the *paneer* and bake in a very hot oven or grill over charcoal or under a very hot grill for about 4 minutes, until the *paneer* starts to turn brown. Serve with sliced raw onion and lemon wedges.

SKEWERED HOME-MADE CHEESE ◷

500 g (1 lb) *paneer*, cut 1 cm (¹/₂ in) thick
2 green or red capsicums (peppers)
2 onions
2 tomatoes
1 cup pineapple wedges
8 button mushrooms
oil to brush the skewers

Marinade:
3 tablespoons plain yogurt
1 tablespoon oil
1 teaspoon tomato paste
1 teaspoon salt
1 teaspoon chilli powder
¹/₂ teaspoon coriander powder
¹/₂ teaspoon cumin powder

Cut the *paneer*, capsicums, onions, tomatoes and pineapple into squares of about 3 cm (1¹/₄ in) and set aside.

Combine all **marinade** ingredients and mix with the *paneer*, vegetables, pineapple and mushrooms. Leave for 1 hour, then thread onto skewers. Cook in a *tandoor*, under a grill or over a hot barbecue until done, brushing with oil half way through cooking.

Opposite:
Skewered Home-made Cheese (left) and Spiced Aubergine (right). Recipe for Spiced Aubergine on page 70. Photograph of Stuffed Home-made Cheese on page 67.

BAIGAN BHARTHA & PINDI CHANNA
Spiced Aubergine & Spiced Chickpeas

Opposite: *Spiced Chickpeas (left) and Spicy Pinto Beans (right). Recipe for Spicy Pinto beans on page 64. Photograph of Spiced Aubergine on page 69.*

SPICED AUBERGINE ⏱

500 g (1 lb) aubergines (eggplant)
1½ tablespoons *ghee* or oil
2 medium-sized onions, finely chopped
3 medium-sized tomatoes, peeled and chopped
2 green chillies, de-seeded and chopped
salt to taste
2½ teaspoons finely chopped coriander leaves

Masala:
1½ teaspoons coriander powder
2 teaspoons cumin powder
1 teaspoon chilli powder
½ teaspoon *garam masala*

Rub aubergine with a little oil and cook over charcoal, until the skin blackens and they are are soft. Peel, then chop the flesh coarsely. Heat *ghee* and sauté onions until light brown. Add **masala** ingredients and cook for a minute. Put in tomatoes and green chilli and sauté for 2-3 minutes. Mix in aubergine and salt and sauté until dry. Serve garnished with chopped coriander leaves.

SPICED CHICKPEAS ⏱

200 g (7 oz) chickpeas
1 tea bag or 1 tablespoon black tea leaves tied in cheese-cloth

6 cups water
6 cm (2½ in) ginger, 2 cm of it shredded finely
2-3 tablespoons oil
4 onions, chopped
2 green chillies, sliced
2 teaspoons finely crushed garlic
3 medium-sized tomatoes, chopped
2 teaspoons coriander powder
1½ teaspoons cumin powder
½ teaspoon turmeric powder
1 teaspoon chilli powder
1 teaspoon salt
2 teaspoons chopped coriander leaves
¼ teaspoon *garam masala*

Soak chickpeas 1 hour, drain and discard liquid. Put chickpeas, 6 cups of fresh water and tea bag into a pan and simmer until chickpeas are tender. Drain, reserving 1 cup of the cooking liquid. Finely chop the remaining ginger. Heat oil and sauté onions until golden, then add garlic, chopped ginger and chillies. Sauté for 5 minutes. Add tomatoes, coriander, cumin, turmeric and chilli powder and sauté over low heat until the oil separates. Add the chickpeas, the reserved cooking liquid, salt and half the coriander leaves. Simmer uncovered until the liquid has been absorbed. Add a pinch of *garam masala* and serve sprinkled with the remaining *garam masala*, coriander leaves and ginger shreds.

AVIAL & MUTTAKOSE THUVIAL

Mixed Vegetables with Yogurt & Cabbage with Coconut

VEGETABLES WITH YOGURT ⏲⏲

150 g (5 oz) drumsticks (optional)
125 g (4 oz) plantains (substitute marrow, chay-
    ote/choko or zucchini/courgette)
125 g (4 oz) potatoes, peeled
125 g (4 oz) carrots, peeled
125 g (4 oz) green beans, cut in 5 cm (2 in)
    lengths
$^{1}/_{2}$ cup whipped yogurt (page 41)
2 teaspoons cumin powder
1 teaspoon turmeric powder

Masala

1 freshly grated coconut, or 2 cups moistened
    desiccated coconut
1 tablespoon cumin seeds, toasted and ground
4–6 green chillies, sliced and de-seeded
$^{1}/_{2}$ teaspoon salt

Prepare the vegetables first. Wash the drumsticks
and cut into 5 cm (2 in) lengths. If using marrow
or zucchini, do not peel; chayote must, however, be
peeled. Cut plantains or substitute, as well as carrots and potatoes into strips about 0.5 cm ($^{1}/_{4}$ in)
square and 5 cm (2 in) long. Blanch in boiling water
for 3 minutes.

Put the vegetables in a pan with just enough
water to cover and simmer, uncovered, until the
vegetables are half-cooked. Add the yogurt, cumin
and turmeric and simmer for another 5-10 minutes,
then add **masala** and mix well. Heat the oil and
sauté the mustard seeds, *dal* and curry leaves until
the spices start to crackle. Mix into the vegetables
and yogurt, stir well and serve immediately.

CABBAGE WITH COCONUT ⏲⏲

1 tablespoon oil
3–4 dried chillies, broken in 2.5 cm (1 in)
    pieces and de-seeded
1 teaspoon husked blackgram *dal* (*urad dal*)
1 teaspoon black mustard seeds
1 sprig curry leaves
500 g (1 lb) cabbage, finely shredded
2 green chillies, sliced
$^{1}/_{2}$ teaspoon chilli powder
$^{1}/_{2}$ teaspoon turmeric powder
$^{1}/_{4}$ cup freshly grated or moistened desiccated
    coconut
salt to taste
1 teaspoon fresh coriander to garnish

Heat the oil and sauté the dried chillies, *dal*, mustard seeds and curry leaves until the spices start to
crackle. Add the cabbage, chillies, chilli powder and
turmeric, stirring to mix well. Cover the pan, lower
the heat and cook gently, stirring from time to time,
until the cabbage is just tender. Add the coconut and
salt to taste. Stir well and season with salt. Garnish
with coriander and serve hot.

DUM ALOO & ALOO POSTA

Spiced Potatoes In Yogurt & Potatoes with Poppy Seeds

SPICED POTATOES IN YOGURT ⏱⏱

500 g (1 lb) baby new potatoes
2 onions, sliced and fried until brown
1 cup plain yogurt
4 black cardamom pods
$\frac{1}{2}$ teaspoon fennel
5 cm (2 in) cinnamon stick
3 tablespoons oil
4 cm (1$\frac{1}{2}$ in) ginger, finely chopped
6 cloves garlic, finely chopped
$\frac{1}{2}$ teaspoon coriander powder
$\frac{1}{2}$ teaspoon cumin powder
$\frac{1}{2}$ teaspoon chilli powder
2 tablespoons melon seeds or cashews, soaked and
    ground to a paste
1 cup water
1 teaspoon salt

Par-boil the potatoes, peel and sauté in oil until golden. Drain and set aside, leaving oil in the pan. Put the onions and half the yogurt in a blender and pureé.

Toast the cardamom, fennel and cinnamon in a dry pan until the spices start to smell fragrant, then blend or grind to a powder. Set aside.

Sauté the ginger and garlic in the oil left from frying the potatoes, then add coriander, cumin and chilli powder and stir for 1 minute. Whisk the remaining yogurt and add together with the nut paste. Heat, then put in the potatoes, water and salt and simmer uncovered until the potatoes are tender. Stir in the reserved ground spices and serve.

POTATOES WITH POPPY SEEDS ⏱⏱

1$\frac{1}{2}$ tablespoons mustard oil
1 bay leaf
250 g (8 oz) potatoes, peeled and cut in 3 cm
    (1$\frac{1}{4}$ in) cubes
$\frac{1}{2}$ teaspoon turmeric
$\frac{1}{2}$ teaspoon chilli powder
2 green chillies, de-seeded and sliced
$\frac{1}{2}$ cup white poppy seeds, soaked in water $\frac{1}{2}$ hour
    and ground to a paste
$\frac{1}{2}$ teaspoon salt

Heat the oil and sauté the bay leaf and potatoes for 2-3 minutes. Add the turmeric, chilli powder and green chillies and sauté for 1 minute. Add the poppy-seed paste, salt and just enough water to cover the potatoes. Cover the pan and simmer until the potatoes are half-cooked, then uncover and simmer, stirring from time to time, until the potatoes are tender and the liquid has dried up.

KADHI PAKORA

Dumplings in Yogurt Sauce

An ideal dish for vegetarians, this Punjabi recipe consists of savoury dumplings made from Bengal gram flour (*besan*) served in a yogurt sauce. ☸☸

Dumplings:

100 g (3½ oz) Bengal gram flour (*besan*)
1 onion, chopped
4 green chillies, de-seeded and chopped
2 cm (¾ in) ginger, finely chopped
1 tablespoon finely chopped coriander leaf
1 teaspoon salt
½ teaspoon carom seeds (*ajwain*)
pinch of bicarbonate of soda
oil for deep frying

Sauce:

125 g (4 oz) Bengal gram flour (*besan*)
1½ cups plain yogurt
3 cups water
1 teaspoon salt
½ teaspoon turmeric powder
2 tablespoons oil
1 sprig curry leaves
½ teaspoon black mustard seeds
3 whole dried chillies
½ teaspoon cumin seeds
¼ teaspoon fenugreek seeds

Mix all the ingredients for the **dumplings** (except for oil) in a bowl, adding enough water to form a sticky consistency. Heat oil until very hot. Wet your hands and take a little batter at a time, shaping it into balls. Heat oil and fry the dumplings, a few at a time, until golden brown. Drain and set aside.

To make the **sauce**, whisk together the flour, yogurt, salt and turmeric. Put in a pan and simmer, stirring from time to time, for about 25 minutes. Heat oil and sauté the curry leaves, mustard seeds, chillies, cumin and fenugreek until the spices start to crackle. Add this to the cooked yogurt sauce, then put in the dumplings and simmer for 3 minutes. Serve hot with rice.

BHINDI BHARWAN & SARSON KA SAAG
Stuffed Okra & Mustard Greens and Spinach

Opposite:
*Mustard Greens
and Spinach (top)
and Stuffed Okra
(bottom).*

STUFFED OKRA ◑◑

500 g (1 lb) okra, washed and dried
3 tablespoons oil
1 teaspoon cumin seeds
1 medium-sized onion, chopped
2 green chillies, de-seeded and chopped
2 cm ($^3/_4$ in) ginger, finely chopped
1 tomato, chopped
pinch of asafoetida powder

Stuffing:

3 teaspoons coriander powder
2 teaspoons turmeric powder
2 teaspoons fennel powder
2 teaspoons dried mango powder
1 teaspoon chilli powder
$^1/_2$ teaspoon salt

Cut the stalk off each okra and make a lengthwise slit. Combine **stuffing** ingredients, mixing well, then stuff a little into each okra. Heat the oil and sauté the okra for 5 minutes. Remove okra from pan and drain, leaving the oil in the pan. Sauté cumin until it starts to crackle. Add onion, chillies and ginger and sauté until the onion turns transparent, then put in the asafoetida and cook for a few seconds. Add tomato and cook until it turns pulpy. Add the fried okra and cook until tender and well coated with the sauce.

MUSTARD GREENS AND SPINACH ◑

1 kg mustard greens, washed, drained and
    shredded
300 g (10 oz) spinach leaves, washed, drained
    and shredded
5 cm (2 in) ginger
6 green chillies, de-seeded and slit lengthwise
1 teaspoon salt
6 cups water
150 g (5 oz) butter
2 tablespoons fine cornmeal
1 teaspoon chilli powder

Put the mustard greens and spinach in a large pan. Cut half the ginger into fine shreds for garnish and keep aside. Chop the remainder finely and add to the pan together with the chillies, salt and water. Bring to the boil, lower heat and simmer, uncovered, stirring from time to time, for at least 1 hour, until the greens are very soft. Purée in a blender and set aside.

Heat 2 tablespoons of the butter in a pan, add the cornmeal and chilli powder and sauté for one minute. Add the puréed greens and the rest of the butter and stir until the greens are heated through and the butter melted. Serve hot garnished with ginger shreds. If liked, fine shreds of tomato and coriander leaf can also be added to garnish.

TANDOORI GOBI
Tandoor-baked Cauliflower

The popularity of *tandoor*-baked dishes is so great in India that new recipes are being developed all the time, including this delicious and simple cauliflower dish. ◷ ◷

600 g (1^1/$_4$ lb) cauliflower
1 teaspoon malt vinegar
1 teaspoon salt
1 teaspoon turmeric powder
^{1}/$_4$ teaspoon mace powder
^{1}/$_4$ teaspoon *chaat masala* (page 39)

Opposite:
*Tandoor-baked
Cauliflower (right
of plate) with
stuffed capsicums
(no recipe).*

Marinade:

1^1/$_2$ cups hung yogurt (page 41)
2 teaspoons crushed garlic
1^1/$_2$ teaspoons crushed ginger
1^1/$_2$ tablespoons chilli paste
^{1}/$_2$ teaspoon *garam masala*
1^1/$_2$ tablespoons oil
2 teaspoons malt vinegar

Divide the cauliflower into 4 florets and prick the stems with a fork to allow the seasonings to penetrate. Heat a pan of water and when boiling, add the cauliflower, vinegar, salt and turmeric. Boil the cauliflower until just tender, drain and allow to cool.

Combine all the **marinade** ingredients and mix in the cauliflower. Leave to marinate for 1^1/$_2$ hours. Cook the cauliflower pieces under a very hot grill or over charcoal until tender and golden brown. Sprinkle with mace and *chaat masala* before serving hot.

Helpful hints: Capsicums (green, red or yellow peppers) can be stuffed with a spicy *paneer* filling, marinated with the same marinade used for *tandoor*-baked cauliflower and baked in a *tandoor* or oven.

MURGH TANDOORI
Tandoori Chicken

Originally from the northwest of India, food baked in a *tandoor* or clay oven heated with charcoal is very popular in restaurants all over the country. Marinated chicken cooked in a *tandoor* achieves an unrivalled succulence and flavour; even using an electric or gas oven, the result is very good. ☉☉

2 spring chickens, each weighing around 650 g (1lb 5 oz)
1 tablespoon chilli paste
2 teaspoons lemon juice
1 teaspoon salt
1 teaspoon *chaat masala* (page 39)
melted butter to baste

Marinade:

2 cups hung yogurt (page 41)
1½ tablespoons chilli paste
1 tablespoon crushed garlic
1 tablespoon crushed ginger
1 tablespoon oil
2 teaspoons lemon juice
1 teaspoon *garam masala*

Make deep gashes on the breast, thighs and drumsticks of each chicken, both inside and outside, to allow the marinade to penetrate. Combine the chilli paste, lemon juice and salt and rub all over the chickens. Refrigerate for 30 minutes.

Prepare the **marinade** by combining the hung yogurt with all other ingredients. Rub this well into the chickens, saving some marinade to rub inside the chest cavity. Marinate chickens for 3–4 hours.

Heat an oven to maximum heat. Put the chickens on a wire rack in a baking dish and baste with a little melted butter. Cook for about 15 minutes, until the chickens are brownish-black and cooked. Sprinkle with *chaat masala* and serve with mint chutney (page 38), onion rings and lemon wedges.

Helpful hints: The chickens can be marinated as much as 24 hours in advance. An alternative method of cooking is to barbecue the chickens over hot charcoal.

MURGH KORMA
Mild Chicken Curry

MILD CHICKEN CURRY

A *korma* is a Mughal creation, rich in fragrant spices and nuts. Chicken *korma* is probably the best known dish prepared in this style, although there are various vegetable, and mutton and lamb *korma*.

🕐 🕐

750 g (1¹/₂ lb) boneless chicken
3 onions, chopped
6–8 cloves garlic, chopped
4 cm (1¹/₂ in) ginger, chopped
100 g (3¹/₂ oz) *ghee* or butter
3 green cardamom pods, bruised
1 black cardamom pods, bruised
4 cm (1¹/₂ in) piece cinnamon
2 bay leaves
1 cup whipped yogurt (page 41)
¹/₄ teaspoon freshly grated nutmeg
1¹/₂ teaspoons white pepper powder
1 teaspoon salt
2 tablespoons cream
¹/₂ teaspoon *garam masala* (page 39)
1 teaspoon chopped coriander leaves to garnish

Nut paste:
3 tablespoons white poppy seeds, soaked and simmered 30 minutes
3 tablespoons unsalted melon seeds, soaked
3 tablespoons *chironji* nuts or blanched almonds
3 tablespoons raw cashew nuts, soaked

Opposite:
Mild Chicken Curry (left) and Butter Chicken (right). Recipe for Butter Chicken on page 82.

Cut the chicken into bite-sized pieces and set aside. Blend together the onions, garlic and ginger to obtain a paste and set aside. Blend the **nut paste** ingredients with just enough water to make a paste and set aside.

Heat the *ghee* and sauté the cardamom, cinnamon and bay leaves for a couple of minutes, then add the blended onion paste. Sauté over very low heat, stirring constantly, until the oil separates, taking care that the mixture does not change colour. Add the yogurt and continue cooking for 15 minutes, stirring from time to time. Add the nutmeg, pepper and chicken and simmer over low heat, uncovered, for 10–15 minutes, until the chicken is tender. Add the nut paste and simmer gently for 3–5 minutes.

Add 1 tablespoon of the cream, salt and half of the *garam masala*, stirring well. Remove from the heat and serve garnished with the remaining cream, *garam masala* and the chopped coriander.

SALLI MURGH
Parsi Chicken Curry

Traditionally served with potato straws, this delicious yet easily prepared Parsi dish is also made with mutton or lamb, when it is known as Salli Boti.
🕐🕐🕐

  3 tablespoons oil
  2 medium-sized onions, sliced
  1 green chilli, sliced
  ¹/₂ teaspoon crushed garlic
  ¹/₂ teaspoon crushed ginger
  ¹/₄ teaspoon turmeric powder
  ¹/₄ teaspoon chilli powder
  2–3 medium-sized tomatoes, chopped
  500 g (1 lb) boneless chicken, cut into 2 cm
    (³/₄ in) pieces
  1 teaspoon salt
  1 teaspoon sugar
  5–6 dried apricots (optional)
  ¹/₄ teaspoon *garam masala* (page 39)
  coriander leaves to garnish

Potato Straws:

  1 kg (2 lb) potatoes, peeled and cut into the
    finest possible shreds
  oil for deep frying
  salt

Heat the oil and sauté the onions until golden brown. Add the chillies, garlic, ginger, turmeric and chilli powder and sauté for 3–4 minutes. Add the tomatoes and cook until pulpy, then put in the chicken and sauté until any moisture which comes out of the chicken dries up. Add salt, sugar and water to cover the chicken and simmer, uncovered, until the oil begins to separate from the gravy. Add the dried apricots and continue cooking until the chicken is tender.

When the curry is ready, prepare the **potato straws**. Dry the shredded potatoes and deep fry in very hot oil until crisp and golden.

To serve, sprinkle the curry with *garam masala* and coriander leaves and top with the potato straws or *salli* sprinkled with salt just before serving to prevent them from becoming soft.

KESARI MURGH & DUM KA MURGH
Saffron Chicken & Rich Chicken Curry

Opposite:
*Saffron Chicken
(top left) and Rich
Chicken Curry
(bottom right)*.

SAFFRON CHICKEN ☺☺☺

1 kg (2 lb) chicken
1 teaspoon salt
3 tablespoons *ghee* or butter
8 cm (3 in) stick cinnamon
4 green cardamom pods, bruised
3 whole cloves
250 g (8 oz) onions, peeled, boiled whole, then puréed
1 teaspoon crushed garlic
2 teaspoons crushed ginger
1 cup whipped yogurt (page 41)
pinch of saffron, soaked in 1 tablespoon warm milk
100 g (3¹/₂ oz) cashew nuts, soaked and ground to a paste
¹/₂ cup cream
coriander leaves to garnish

Debone the chicken and sprinkle with salt. Set aside. Heat *ghee* and sauté cinnamon, cardamom and cloves for a minute, then add puréed onions, garlic and ginger and continue sautéing until they begin to take colour. Add the yogurt and saffron and cook for 15 minutes, stirring occasionally. Add the chicken, simmer for 5 minutes, then add the cashew nut paste and blend well. Simmer until the chicken is tender. Add the cream, heat through and serve garnished with coriander leaves.

RICH CHICKEN CURRY ☺☺☺

1 whole chicken, weighing about 1 kg (2 lb)
¹/₄ cup oil
4 onions, sliced
2 cups plain yogurt
1 cup mixed nuts (almonds, cashews and *chironji*), soaked and ground to a paste
2 teaspoons crushed garlic
2 teaspoons crushed ginger
pinch of saffron, soaked in 1 tablespoon warm milk
few drops rose essence
4 cloves
3 green cardamom pods, bruised
1 bay leaf
1 teaspoon salt

Choose a heavy casserole dish or saucepan with a well fitting lid. Cut the chicken into 4 pieces and set aside. Heat the oil and gently fry the onions until brown. Drain the onions, reserving 1 tablespoon of the oil. Blend the yogurt and onions together to make a paste, then combine this with the chicken, nut paste, garlic, ginger, saffron and rose essence.

Heat the reserved tablespoon of oil and sauté the cloves, cardamoms and bay leaf for a couple of minutes, then add the chicken and salt. Stir to mix well. Make a flour and water paste and seal the lid onto the casserole or saucepan. Cook over very low heat or in a slow oven for about 40 minutes. Uncover only just before serving.

RAAN PATHANI
Braised Lamb Leg

Baby lamb not more than two or three months old is normally used for this succulent dish, each leg weighing around 600 g (1¼ lb). If baby lamb is not available, a larger lamb leg can be used. The cooked meat should be so tender that it can be served with a spoon. ☺☺☺

1 lamb leg, weighing not more than 1.25 kg (3 lb)
2 tablespoons oil
6 tablespoons tomato paste
1 teaspoon salt

Marinade:

1 teaspoon crushed garlic
1 teaspoon crushed ginger
1 teaspoon chilli paste
1 tablespoon oil

Masala:

4–5 onions, sliced
1 teaspoon crushed garlic
1 teaspoon crushed ginger
1 teaspoon chilli paste
2 teaspoons coriander powder
1 teaspoon cumin powder
¾ teaspoon turmeric powder

Whole Spices:

3 cloves
4 green cardamom pods, bruised
3 black cardamom pods, bruised
2 cinnamon sticks, each 5 cm (2 in)
2 whole star anise
1 bay leaf

Make deep slashes in the lamb to allow the spices to penetrate. Combine the **marinade** ingredients, rub into the lamb and leave aside for 3–4 hours.

Combine the *masala* ingredients and blend to obtain a paste. Heat 2 tablespoons oil in a casserole dish or heavy pan just large enough to hold the lamb leg. Sauté the **whole spices** for 2–3 minutes, then add the ground *masala* and sauté until the oil separates. Add the tomato paste and salt, heat and put in the lamb. Cook over very low heat or in an oven (about 150°C/300°F) for about 2 hours, or until the lamb is very tender, turning once or twice.

Before serving, put the cooked lamb over a charcoal fire or under a very hot grill for a few minutes, turning so that the sauce coating dries slightly. Serve with Indian bread and rice.

SORPOTEL

Goan Spiced Pork and Liver

The Goan style of cooking pork involves vinegar and spices as preservatives. Traditional Sorpotel used every part of the pig: the liver, kidneys, tongue, ears and blood. Each household has its own version, and the following is an authentic family recipe. *Feni*, a liquor made from cashews, is used in Goa, but brandy can be substituted. ☺☺☺

> 500 g (1 lb) pork with fat and skin, in one
>   piece
> 250 g (8 oz) pig's liver, in one piece
> 1–2 teaspoons chilli powder
> $\frac{1}{2}$ teaspoon turmeric powder
> $\frac{1}{2}$ teaspoon cinnamon powder
> 12 black peppercorns
> 12 cloves
> 6 green cardamon pods
> 1 cup vinegar, or more to taste
> 4 cloves garlic
> 2 onions, chopped
> 2 tomatoes, chopped
> 1 teaspoon sugar
> 2 tablespoons *feni or* brandy
> salt to taste

Boil meat and liver separately, with just enough water to just cover, for 15 minutes. Remove and reserve liquids. Cut meat and liver into 1 cm ($\frac{1}{2}$ in) cubes. Heat a dry pan and fry the diced meat, stirring frequently, until browned. (The lard that comes out of the fat pork should be sufficient to cook it.) Drain and set aside, keeping the lard in the pan.

Grind or blend the turmeric powder, cinnamon, pepper, cloves and cardamoms together with just enough vinegar to make a thick paste.

Using the lard left in the pan, fry the garlic and onions until brown, then add the tomatoes and cook until pulpy. Add the spice paste and cook 5 minutes. Add the reserved liquids from the meat and liver, and put in the fried cubes of pork and liver. Simmer very slowly for 15 minutes, then add sugar, *feni* or brandy and a cup or more of vinegar. Simmer until tender, stirring occasionally. The resultant dish should have a curry-like gravy.

Helpful hints: Vinegar made from coconut toddy is normally used; if you cannot obtain coconut vinegar (also used in Filipino cooking), use rice vinegar, or cider vinegar diluted with 1 part of water to 4 parts of vinegar. This dish can be made at least two or three days in advance; Goans insist it tastes better after a few days, when the flavours have had a chance to blend and penetrate the meat.

VINDALOO

Goan Pork Curry

This dish was once carried on sea voyages. No water is used in the preparation and the layer of fat on the top helps seal out air and preserve the meat. Vindaloos have traditionally been very pungent, although this recipe should cause just a gentle sweat. Choose pork that has some fat on it. ② ②

500 g (1 lb) pork, cut in 2 cm (³/₄ in) cubes
8 cloves garlic
3 teaspoons chilli powder
4 green chillies
1 teaspoon black peppercorns
2.5 cm (1 in) fresh ginger, finely chopped
1 teaspoon cumin seeds
2 onions, chopped
1 cup coconut vinegar, (see *Helpful hint*, page 94)
salt to taste
1 teaspoon sugar
2 tablespoons *feni or* brandy

Fry the pork in its own fat for 5 minutes. While the pork is frying, grind or blend the garlic, chilli powder, chillies, pepper, ginger and cumin seeds with vinegar to a thick paste.

Take 1 tablespoon of the lard or fat that runs out from the pork and put in a separate pan. Sauté the onions until golden brown, then add the ground ingredients and fry 5 minutes. Add this mixture to the pork, stir and add vinegar and salt. Simmer very gently for 3 hours until the gravy is very thick, then add sugar and *feni or* brandy.

AATIRACHI & MASS KE TIKKA
Kerala Lamb Curry & Lamb Kebabs

KERALA LAMB CURRY ☻☻☻

2 tablespoons oil
6 green cardamom pods, bruised
$^1/_2$ teaspoon black peppercorns
8–10 shallots, sliced
600 g (1$^1/_4$ lb) boneless lamb, cut in 2.5 cm (1 in) cubes
$^1/_2$ teaspoon salt
$^3/_4$ cup water
fresh coriander leaf to garnish

Masala:

3 onions, chopped
2 cm ($^3/_4$ in) ginger, chopped
4–6 cloves garlic, chopped
0.5 cm ($^1/_4$ in) fresh turmeric or $^1/_2$ teaspoon turmeric powder
2 ripes tomatoes, chopped
4–6 dried chillies, broken and soaked to soften
2 green chillies, chopped
6 green cardamom pods
1 teaspoon black mustard seeds
$^1/_2$ teaspoon black peppercorns

Process or blend the **masala** ingredients to make a paste. Keep aside.

Heat oil and fry the green cardamoms and peppercorns for 2 minutes. Add the shallots and sauté until they turn golden brown. Put in the meat and sauté until brown, then add the *masala* and sauté

Opposite: *Kerala Lamb Curry*. *Photograph of Lamb Kebabs on page 103.*

on low heat for 10–15 minutes. Add the salt and water, cover the pan and cook gently until the meat is tender. Garnish with coriander leaf and serve with rice or Flaky Fried Bread (page 56).

LAMB KEBABS ☻☻

600 g (1$^1/_4$ lb) boneless lamb
1$^1/_2$ cups hung yogurt (page 41)
2$^1/_2$ teaspoons chilli paste
2 teaspoons crushed garlic
1 teaspoon crushed ginger
2 teaspoons cumin seeds, toasted and ground
$^1/_2$ teaspoon mace powder
$^1/_2$ teaspoon *garam masala* (page 39)
1 teaspoon salt
1$^1/_2$ tablespoons oil
2 teaspoons lemon juice
oil for basting

Cut the meat into cubes of about 3 cm (1$^1/_4$ in) and prick all over with a fork. Mix all other ingredients (except oil for basting) together and add the meat, stirring to coat well. Leave to marinate in the refrigerator for a minimum of 4 hours. Thread the meat onto skewers and cook over a charcoal fire or under a very hot grill for 3–4 minutes. Brush the meat with oil, turn and cook until done. Serve hot.

HYDERABADI KACCHI BIRYANI
Spiced Mutton with Rice

A classic recipe from the kitchens of the Nizams or Muslim rulers of Hyderabad. 🕐 🕐

- 250 g (8 oz) boneless lamb or mutton, cut in 4 cm (1½ in) cubes
- 250 g (8 oz) lamb or mutton with bone, chopped the same size as the boneless lamb
- 2 tablespoons ghee or butter
- 1 teaspoon cumin seeds
- 5 cloves
- 8 cm (3 in) cinnamon stick
- 2 bay leaves
- 2 black cardamon pods, bruised
- 4 green cardamon pods, bruised
- 3–4 green chillies, slit lengthwise
- 1 medium-sized onion, sliced
- 1 teaspoon salt

Rice:

- 2 green cardamom pods, bruised
- 3 cloves
- 3 cm (1½ in) cinnamon stick
- 1 bay leaf
- 1 blade of mace
- a few rose petals or 2–3 drops of rose essence
- 500 g (1 lb) long-grain rice, soaked 1 hour and drained

Marinade:

- 1 cup hung yogurt (page 41)
- juice of 2 lemons
- 1 teaspoon crushed ginger
- 1 teaspoon crushed garlic
- 1½ teaspoons *garam masala* (page 39)
- 1 teaspoon coriander powder
- 1 teaspoon chilli powder
- ¼ teaspoon turmeric powder
- ½ cup mint leaves
- 1½ cup coriander leaves

Combine all **marinade** ingredients. Mix well with the meat and leave to marinate for at least 3 hours.

Cook the **rice**. Put the spices and seasonings into a large pan full of water and bring to the boil. Add the rice and boil rapidly for 3 minutes, until just half-cooked, then drain thoroughly, discarding the whole spices. Keep rice aside.

Choose a heavy bottomed pan or casserole dish and put it over moderate heat with the *ghee*. Sauté the spices until they begin to crackle, then add the chillies and onion and sauté until the onions are light brown. Add the salt and meat together with its marinade, stir and spread the rice on top.

Make a flour-and-water paste to seal on the lid of the pan. Put the pan over high heat for 5–7 minutes, then reduce the heat as low as possible. If you are using a gas flame, use a heat-diffusing mat to spread the heat rather than have it concentrated in the centre of the pan. Leave the pan over minimum heat for 45 minutes, then serve.

KEEMA KOFTA

Spicy Meatballs

SPICY MEATBALLS

A speciality of Uttar Pradesh region, these meatballs are bathed in a sauce enriched with pounded cashews and almonds. In India, the meat would be bought in one piece, mixed well with the seasonings and then taken to a shop to be put through a mincer. A similar effect can be achieved in a Western kitchen by using a food processor. ☹ ☹ ☹

Opposite:
Lamb Kebas (left) and Spicy Meatballs (right). Recipe for Lamb Kebabs on page 98.

500 g (1 lb) lean lamb
3 green chillies, sliced
1 tablespoon chopped coriander leaves
1 cm ($^{1}/_{2}$ in) ginger, finely chopped
$^{1}/_{4}$ teaspoon powdered cloves
$^{1}/_{4}$ teaspoon powdered mace
a pinch of *garam masala*
$^{1}/_{2}$ teaspoon salt
1 tablespoon *ghee* or butter

Sauce:

2 tablespoons raw cashews
2 tablespoons blanched almonds
1 heaped tablespoon *ghee* or butter
4 onions, finely chopped
$^{3}/_{4}$ teaspoon crushed garlic
$^{3}/_{4}$ teaspoon crushed ginger
$^{1}/_{4}$ teaspon turmeric powder
$^{1}/_{2}$ teaspoon chilli powder

3 tomatoes, finely chopped or blended
$^{1}/_{4}$ cup whipped yogurt (page 41)
1 tablespoon chopped mint leaves
salt to taste
pinch of *garam masala*

Cut the lamb into cubes and mix in a bowl with the chillies, coriander, ginger, spices and salt, keeping the *ghee* aside. Blend seasoned meat in a food processor until very finely ground. Shape into balls about 2 cm ($^{3}/_{4}$ in) in diameter and sauté in *ghee* or butter until browned. Keep aside.

Make the **sauce.** Soak the cashews and almonds in hot water to cover for about 10 minutes, then pound or process to make a paste. Heat the *ghee* and sauté the onions until golden. Add the garlic, ginger, turmeric and chilli powder and sauté until the oil separates. Add the tomatoes and cook until they become pulpy. Add the yogurt and nut paste and simmer over low heat until the oil separates.

Add the meat balls, cover the pan and simmer for 5-7 minutes, stirring gently from time to time. Add half the chopped mint and salt to taste, then garnish with the remaining mint and *garam masala*.

MAAS KOLHAPURI
Spicy Hot Mutton Curry

Food from Kolhapur in Maharashtra state is invariably laden with chillies and extremely hot. However, the rich flavour of the curry will still come through if you adjust the amount of chilli paste to suit your taste. ☺ ☺ ☺

2 tablespoons oil
4 onions, sliced
2$^1/_2$ teaspoons crushed garlic
1 teaspoon crushed ginger
2$^1/_2$ teaspoons chilli paste
1 teaspoon coriander powder
$^1/_2$ teaspoon turmeric powder
1 kg (2 lb) boneless mutton or lamb, cut in 2.5 cm (1 in) cubes
4 ripe tomatoes, chopped
1 teaspoon salt
1$^1/_2$ cups water
3–4 whole dried chillies, fried in oil to garnish
very finely shredded ginger to garnish

Masala:

1$^1/_2$ tablespoons coriander seeds
2 blades mace
4 cloves
2 teaspoons black peppercorns
8 cm (3 in) cinnamon stick
3 dried red chillies, broken in 2.5 cm (1 in) pieces
1 cup freshly grated coconut

Prepare the **masala** by putting all ingredients except the coconut in a pan and toasting over low heat until they start to smell fragrant. Allow to cool slightly, then grind to a powder. Add the coconut and grind to mix well. Keep aside.

Heat oil and sauté onion until golden brown. Add the ginger, garlic and chilli paste and cook until it smells fragrant, then add the coriander and turmeric and sauté for another couple of minutes.

Add the meat and sauté until it has browned all over. Put in the **masala** paste and sauté for about 15 minutes, then add the tomatoes and salt. Add water and cook over low heat, stirring from time to time, until the meat is tender. Garnish with fried chillies and ginger and serve with white rice.

DHANSAK DAL
Mixed Lentils, Vegetables & Lamb

This is a favourite among India's Parsi community, who are renowned meat eaters. *Dhansak*, a mixture of puréed *dal*, vegetables and meat, is a substantial one-dish meal traditionally served with brown rice, lemon wedges and *Kachumber*. ☻☻☻

500 g (1 lb) yellow (*tuvar*) *dal*
100 g (3½ oz) red lentils (*masoor dal*)
100 g (3½ oz) mung peas (*moong dal*)
¼ cup oil
2 onions, sliced
¾ teaspoon turmeric powder
500 g (1 lb) lamb, cut in 2.5 cm (1 in) cubes
1 teaspoon coriander powder
1 teaspoon cumin powder
1 small aubergine (eggplant), peeled and diced
250 g (8 oz) pumpkin, peeled and diced
6 cups water
1 teaspoon salt
1 tablespoon oil
500 g (1 lb) spinach

Masala:
1 tablespoon cumin seeds
1 tablespoon coriander seeds
5 cm (2 in) cinnamon stick
5 green cardamom pods
¼ teaspoon black peppercorns
8 cloves garlic
5 cm (2 in) ginger
7 red chillies

Wash the lentils and peas and soak overnight. Drain and set aside. Grind all ingredients for the **masala**, adding just enough water to make a firm paste. Set aside.

Heat oil and fry the onions until golden brown. Add the ground *masala*, turmeric powder, coriander and cumin powders and fry gently for about 5 minutes, stirring frequently. Add the lamb and continue cooking until all the liquid that comes out of the meat has dried up.

Add the drained lentils, aubergine and pumpkin and mix well. Gradually add water, stirring well, then season with salt and bring to the boil. Cover, reduce heat and simmer gently until the meat is tender. Remove the meat and set aside. Put the lentil and vegetable mix into a food processor and make a purée, or mash by hand. Return the meat to the mixture.

Heat oil and add the spinach. Sauté until the leaves have wilted, then add to the *dal* mixture and cook over low heat for 5 minutes. Garnish with lemon wedges and serve hot with brown rice and *Kachumber* (page 40).

MAKAI GOSHT

Lamb and Corn Curry

Corn, more commonly used in Rajasthan than other regons of India, is cooked with lamb in this unusual curry. Use fresh raw corn if possible, or failing that, frozen sweetcorn; if forced to use canned corn, add only towards the end of cooking. ♪♪♪

1$^1\!/_2$ tablespoons *ghee* or oil
2 cloves
2 green cardamom pods, bruised
1 cm ($^1\!/_2$ in) cinnamon stick
1 blade mace
1 kg (2 lb) boneless lamb, cut in 3 cm (1$^1\!/_4$ in) cubes
4 onions, chopped
5 cm (2 in) ginger, chopped
6 cloves garlic, chopped
3 green chillies, de-seeded and chopped
$^1\!/_2$ teaspoon turmeric powder
$^1\!/_2$ teaspoon chilli powder
3 tablespoons coriander seeds, toasted and ground
100 g (3$^1\!/_2$ oz) sweetcorn kernels, preferably fresh (see above)
1 cup plain yogurt
1 teaspoon salt
3 tablespoons cashews, soaked and ground to a paste (optional)
$^1\!/_3$ cup cream
coriander leaf to garnish
finely shredded ginger to garnish

Heat the *ghee* or oil and sauté the cloves, cardamoms, cinnamon and mace. Add the lamb and sauté until all the liquid has dried up. Blend the onions, ginger and garlic to a paste and add this to the lamb together with the green chllies, turmeric, chilli power and coriander.

Sauté until the oil separates, then put in the fresh or frozen sweetcorn kernels, yogurt, water to just cover the meat, salt and cashew-nut paste. Simmer uncovered until the meat is tender and the gravy has thickened. If using canned sweetcorn, add 5 minutes before the end of cooking time.

Add the cream, heat through and serve garnished with coriander and ginger shreds.

THANDI AJWAINI MACCHI
Fish Pâté in Pastry

Fish goes particularly well with carom, a spice which comes from the same family as cumin and parsley. This elegant recipe from Hyderabad, where Continental cooks were once employed by the aristocracy, calls for expensive seasonings such as saffron and pistachios and cooks the pâté European-style, wrapped in pastry. ☺ ☺ ☺

Fish Pâté:

- 1 kg (2 lb) white fish (freshwater if possible), skinned, boned and cubed
- 2 eggs
- 3 tablespoons full-cream milk powder
- 2 tablespoons butter
- 1 teaspoon carom seeds (*ajwain*)
- 2 tablepsoons chopped coriander leaf
- 2 tablespoon coarsely chopped spring onion
- ¹/₂ teaspoon salt
- ¹/₄ teaspoon white pepper powder
- 1 tablespoon skinned pistachio nuts, chopped
- pinch of saffron threads, soaked in warm milk
- 1 egg, beaten with 2 teaspoons water

Pastry:

- 500 g (1 lb) plain white flour
- 150 g (5 oz) *ghee* or butter
- 2 tablespoons iced water
- 3 tablespoons oil
- pinch of salt

Combine all ingredients for the pâté except pistachios, saffron and egg wash. Process in a blender until fine, then stir in the pistachios and saffron (together with the soaking liquid). Mix well and chill in the fridge for at least 1 hour.

Make a dough by combining all the **pastry** ingredients, then roll it out to a thickness of 25 mm (¹/₈ in). Mould the fish pâté mixture into a cylinder or triangle if preferred and place on the centre of the pastry. Wrap the pastry around to enclose the fish and apply egg wash on all sides with a brush. Decorate the top with trimmings of dough, applying egg wash on trimmings. Bake in a medium oven (180°C/350°F) for 30 minutes.

Allow to cool, then chill in the fridge. Cut into thin slices. Serve with mint & coriander chutney (page 38) and lemon wedges as an appetiser, or serve together with a salad as a light meal.

MACHCHI AMRITSARI

Fish in Seasoned Batter

India's Sikhs are very fond of freshwater fish. This recipe from Amritsar, where the Sikh's holiest shrine, the Golden Temple, is located, is a tangy combination of marinated fish coated in batter and deep fried until crisp. ☻☻

1 kg (2 lb) white fish cutlets, or fish fillets if
    cutlets not available
oil for deep frying
¹/₂ teaspoon *chaat masala* (page 39)
pinch of *garam masala* (page 39)

Batter:

1¹/₂ tablespoons oil
150 g (5 oz) Bengal gram flour (*besan*)
1 egg, lightly beaten
¹/₂ teaspoon crushed garlic
¹/₂ teaspoon crushed ginger
¹/₂ teaspoon chilli powder
1 teaspoon carom seeds (*ajwain*), rubbed
    slightly with the hand
1 teaspoon salt
1 teaspoon *chaat masala* (page 39)
1 tablespoon chopped coriander leaves
1–2 green chillies, de-seeded and chopped
2 teaspoons lemon juice

Prepare the **batter** first by heating the oil and mixing in the Bengal gram flour. Cook for 1 minute, stirring, then remove from the heat and allow to cool. Mix in all other batter ingredients and add water if necessary to make a very thick batter.

Combine the fish and batter and let stand for 20 minutes. Heat oil and fry the fish until the batter is crisp and the fish cooked. Sprinkle with both lots of *masala* and serve hot.

Helpful hint: To save time, the batter can be made up to 1 day in advance and kept refrigerated. Stir well before using.

MACHER JHOL & KANJU MASALA
Bengali Fish Curry & Kerala Prawn Curry

BENGALI FISH CURRY ⊘⊘

750 g (1¹/₂ lb) white fish cutlets or fillets
2 teaspoons salt
1 teaspoon turmeric
mustard oil for shallow frying
1 large potato, cut in wedges
1 small aubergine (eggplant), sliced
4 cups water
4 green chillies, de-seeded and slit lengthwise

Masala:
¹/₂ teaspoon cumin seeds
¹/₂ teaspoon fennel seeds
¹/₂ teaspoon black mustard seeds
¹/₄ teaspoon fenugreek seeds
¹/₄ teaspoon nigella seeds (*kalonji*)

Opposite:
*Bengali Fish
Curry.
Photograph of
Kerala Prawn
Curry is on
page 117.*

Wipe the fish dry, sprinkle both sides with salt and turmeric and set aside to marinate for 5 minutes. Heat oil in a pan and sauté the fish until golden brown on both sides and cooked through. Set fish aside. Using the same oil, sauté the **masala** spices until they start to crackle. Add the potato and aubergine and sauté until well coated with the spices. Put in the water and simmer until the vegetables are tender. Add fish and chillies and heat through. Serve with plain rice.

KERALA PRAWN CURRY ⊘⊘⊘

3 dried chillies, torn and soaked in water to
    soften
2 teaspoons black peppercorns
1 teaspoon cumin seeds
¹/₂ teaspoon turmeric powder
2 cm (³/₄ in) ginger, chopped
4–6 cloves garlic, chopped
¹/₃ cup oil
600 g (1¹/₄ lb) prawns, peeled and deveined
2 sprigs curry leaves
¹/₂ teaspoon black mustard seeds
100 g (3¹/₂ oz) onions, sliced
3 tablespoons tamarind pulp, soaked in 2 cups
    water and strained
¹/₂ teaspoon salt

Grind or blend chillies, peppercorns, cumin, turmeric, ginger and garlic together, adding just a little of the oil if necessary to keep the blades of your blender turning. Mix with prawns and set aside.

Heat oil and fry the curry leaves and mustard seeds until the mustard seeds begin to pop. Add the sliced onion and cook until golden brown. Add the prawns and sauté until they change colour, then put in the tamarind juice and salt. Simmer for about 5 minutes until the prawns are cooked.

MEEN MOLEE
Fish in Coconut Milk

FISH IN COCONUT MILK ☺☺

4 whole small pomfret, weighing about 350 g
    (11 oz) each, or 750 g white fish fillets or
    steaks
$\frac{1}{2}$ teaspoon turmeric powder
1 teaspoon chilli powder
1 teaspoon salt
3 tablespoons oil
2 cm ($\frac{3}{4}$ in) ginger, finely chopped
6–8 cloves garlic, finely chopped
6 green chillies, de-seeded and slit lengthwise
6 green cardamom pods, bruised
3 onions, sliced
2 teaspoons coriander powder
$1\frac{1}{2}$ cups thin coconut milk
banana leaf (optional)
3 sprigs curry leaves
1 cup thick coconut milk
1 teaspoon black mustard seeds
1 teaspoon lime or lemon juice

Opposite:
Fish in Coconut
Milk (right) and
Kerala Prawn
Curry (left).
Recipe for Kerala
Prawn Curry on
page 114.

Clean pomfret and cut gashes on both sides to allow the spices to penetrate. Sprinkle fish with turmeric powder, chilli powder and salt and marinate for 5 minutes. Heat the oil and pan fry the pomfret on both sides until golden. Remove and set aside.

Sauté ginger, garlic, green chillies, cardamoms and onions. Add coriander powder and thin coconut milk and heat, stirring.

Line the bottom of a wide, thick bottomed pan with the banana leaf; this is optional, but adds a delicate flavour to the curry. Place curry leaves and fish on top and pour the prepared gravy on top. Bring to the boil, uncovered, then simmer until the fish is cooked.

Add the thick coconut milk and heat through, but do not allow to boil. Heat 1 teaspoon oil and fry the mustard seeds until they start to pop. Pour this into the fish, add the lemon juice and serve.

MACHER KALIA & CHINGDI MACHER

Spicy Fried Fish & Creamy Prawn Curry

SPICY FRIED FISH ⏱⏱

500 g (1 lb) white fish cutlets
½ teaspoon turmeric powder
1 teaspoon salt
mustard oil for shallow frying
1 teaspoon black mustard seeds
2 green chillies, slit lengthwise
1 teaspoon coriander powder
1 teaspoon cumin powder
½–1 teaspoon chilli powder
½ cup plain yogurt

Masala:

2 onions, chopped
1 cm (½ in) ginger, chopped
4 cloves garlic, chopped
1 tomato, chopped

CREAMY PRAWN CURRY ⏱⏱⏱

2 cm (¾ in) ginger
6 cloves garlic
½ teaspoon cumin seeds
3 tablespoons mustard oil
1 bay leaf
4 cloves
5 cm (2 in) cinnamon
4 green cardamom pods, bruised
1 large onion, chopped
4 green chillies, de-seeded and chopped
salt to taste
½ cup water
500 g (1 lb) prawns, peeled and deveined
1 cup thick coconut milk
1 teaspoon sugar
chopped coriander leaf to garnish

Sprinkle the fish with turmeric powder and salt and marinate for 5 minutes. Heat oil and fry the fish until golden. Remove, drain and set fish aside. Remove all but 2 tablespoons of oil from the pan.

Blend the **masala** ingredients to a paste. In the oil remaining in the pan, sauté the mustard seeds and chillies for 2 minutes. Add coriander, cumin and chilli powders as well as the *masala* paste and sauté until fragrant. Add yogurt and cook until the oil starts to separate. Add fish and cook until tender.

Pound the ginger, garlic and cumin. Heat oil and sauté the bay leaf, cloves, cinnamon and cardamom until fragrant. Add onion and sauté gently for 5 minutes. Add green chilli and ginger-garlic-cumin paste. Sauté for 2 minutes, then add salt and water. Simmer uncovered for 5 minutes, then put in the prawns and simmer for 3 minutes. Add coconut milk and simmer gently, stirring occasionally, until the prawns are tender. Add sugar, stir and serve garnished with coriander leaves.

NANDU KARI

Crab Curry

This dish comes from Mangalore, on the southwest coast, an area renowned for its liking for both fish and coconuts. This succulent curry uses coconut milk plus freshly grated coconut for a wonderfully rich gravy. ⏱ ⏱

4 live crabs, each weighing about 250–300 g (8–10 oz)
2 tablespoons oil
1 teaspoon black mustard seeds
3 sprigs curry leaves
2 bay leaves
3 green chillies, halved lengthwise
pinch of asafoetida powder
3 onions, sliced
$^1/_4$ teaspoon turmeric powder
1 teaspoon chilli powder
2 tomatoes, chopped
1 cup coconut milk
salt to taste
$^1/_4$ cup freshly grated or moistened desiccated coconut

Plunge crabs in a large pan of boiling water for 2-3 minutes, then drain and chop into large pieces, cracking the shell to allow the flavourings to penetrate. Clean and discard the spongey grey matter. Drain the crabs thoroughly.

Heat oil in a wok and fry mustard seeds until they start popping. Add the curry and bay leaves and green chillies and sauté gently for 1 minute, before adding the asafoetida. Add onions and cook until the onion is transparent, then sprinkle in turmeric and chilli powders. Sauté for 1 minute, then add the crab pieces and tomatoes. Cover the wok and cook, without adding water, stirring occasionally. When the crab is cooked (about 10 minutes), add the coconut milk and salt. Bring just to the boil, stirring constantly, then add the grated coconut and serve with plain steamed rice.

KULFI & GULAB JAMUN
Indian Ice Cream & Fried Milk Balls in Syrup

INDIAN ICE CREAM ☺☺☺

2 litres (8 cups) full-fat milk
125 g (4 oz) sugar
1–2 tablespoons skinned pistacho nuts, chopped

Falooda:
200 g (7 oz) cornflour
4 cups water

To make the ice cream, put the milk into a wide, heavy pan and cook over very low heat, stirring constantly until the milk has thickened and reduced to about 2 cups. Stir the sides of the pan constantly to prevent the milk from burning. Add the sugar and pistachios and allow to cool. Freeze in individual metal containers such as jelly moulds. Unmould and serve with a garnish of *Falooda*.

To make the **Falooda**, dissolve the cornflour in 1 cup of water. Heat the remaining water in a pan, add the blended cornflour and cook to make a thick jell. While the mixture is still hot, put into a press capable of making fine threads the size of vermicelli. Fill a bowl full of cold water right up to the brim and set the press over the water so that when the *Falooda* is pushed through the press, it immediately touches the water. Push all the jell through the press. Store the *falooda* in water until required. Drain and serve with the ice cream.

FRIED MILK BALLS IN SYRUP ☺☺

1 kg (2 lb) *khoa* (page 41)
200 g (7 oz) *chenna* (page 41)
2 tablespoons plain flour
pinch of bicarbonate of soda
2 tablespoons skinned pistachio nuts, chopped
oil for deep frying

Syrup:
2.5 kg sugar
1½ litres (6 cups) water

Make the **syrup** by boiling the water and sugar together, stirring from time to time, for about 10 minutes until thickened slightly. Keep aside.

Crumble the *khoa* and mix with *chenna*, flour, bicarbonate of soda and pistachios to make a soft dough. Make one very small ball for testing the consistency. Heat oil until moderately hot and fry the ball; if it breaks apart, the mixture is too moist and a little more plain flour should be mixed in to the dough. When the mixture is the correct consistency, shape it into balls about 6 cm (2½ in) in diameter and deep fry, a few at a time, until golden brown. Drain the fried balls and put into the warm syrup. Serve warm or at room temperature.

SHRIKAND

Sweet Yogurt with Saffron

In India, this Gujarati favourite is always served with deep-fried bread (*puri*). As it is so rich and substantial, you may prefer it simply on its own. If liked, the saffron can be omitted and about ¹/₂ cup concentrated mango pulp added for a different flavour. ⏱

1¹/₂ litres (6 cups) plain yogurt
125 g (4 oz) castor or icing sugar
1 tablespoon skinned pistacho nuts, chopped
2 teaspoons *chironji* nuts, hazelnuts or almonds, chopped
1/4 teaspoon cardamom powder
pinch of saffron threads, soaked in a little hot milk

Put the yogurt into a large sieve or colander lined with wet cheesecloth and allow to drain for 6-8 hours, until it is relatively firm.

Sprinkle the drained yogurt with sugar, stirring to dissolve it, then push the mixture through a fine sieve to obtain a silken smooth texture. Add half of the pistachos, the *chironji* nuts, cardamom and saffron (or mango pulp, if preferred). Mix and chill before serving garnished with the remaining pistachios. Additional saffron can be used for garnishing if liked.

RASGULLA

Cream Cheese Balls in Syrup

Soft home-made cream cheese or *chenna* is shaped into balls and simmered in syrup to make a simple but richly satisfying dessert. An extravagant touch in the form of pure silver beaten into the finest possible sheets is sometimes added as a garnish on special occasions in India. ☺ ☺

250 g (8 oz) *chenna* (page 41)
1 teaspoon flour

Syrup:
1 kg (2 lb) sugar
3 cups water

Make the **syrup** by bringing the sugar and water to the boil. Turn off the heat and set aside.

Combine the *chenna* and flour and shape into balls. Reheat the syrup and when it is boiling, add the balls and simmer for about 20 minutes. Add another 2 tablespoons of water to the syrup every 5 minutes to replace water lost by evaporation; this is essential to avoid having the syrup become too thick. When the cream cheese balls are cooked, remove from the syrup, drain and keep covered in water until required. Serve with a spoonful or two of the syrup poured over the top.

CHANNA DAL PAYASAM & KHEER

Southern Indian Dessert & Rich Rice Pudding

SOUTHERN INDIAN DESSERT

Universally popular in the south of India, *Payasam* is made of sweetened milk with a variety of nuts, *dal*, pearl sago or even wheat-flour vermicelli added. This version uses Bengal gram (*channa dal*) and is enriched with coconut milk. ☺☺

2 tablespoons split Bengal gram
2 cups milk
$^1\!/_2$ cup thick coconut milk
75 g (2$^1\!/_2$ oz) palm sugar (*jaggery*)
2 tablespoons *ghee*
1–2 green cardamom pods, bruised
1 tablespoon raw cashew nuts, coarsely chopped
1 tablespoon raisins or sultanas

Wash the Bengal gram and simmer with 1 cup of water until half cooked. Add the milk and simmer until the gram is very soft, then add the coconut milk and palm sugar. Cook, stirring frequently, until the mixture thickens. Heat the *ghee* and sauté the cashew nuts and raisins until golden brown, then add to the cooked mixture. Although *Payasam* is normally served warm or at room temperature, it can be chilled if preferred.

RICH RICE PUDDING

A northern favourite, this rice pudding is very different from the bland version which countless children had to endure in their homes or boarding schools in Britain. ☺☺

$^1\!/_2$ cup long-grain rice, washed and drained
3 cups milk
2–3 green cardamom pods, bruised
2 tablespoons blanched slivered almonds
pinch of saffron threads, soaked in a little hot milk
1 tablepsoon skinned pistachio nuts, chopped
1 tablespoon raisins (optional)
3–4 tablespoons sugar

Put the rice, milk and cardamom into a pan, bring to the boil and simmer gently until the rice is soft and the grains are starting to break up. Add the almonds, saffron, pistachios and raisins (if using) and simmer for 3–4 minutes. Add the sugar and stir until completely dissolved. Remove from heat and serve either warm or chilled.

Index

Notes